The Adventures of a Maryknoll Priest in Africa

Bringing the Good News of Jesus Christ to the Youth of Tanzania, East Africa

Father Marvin Deutsch M.M.

Bringing the Good News of Jesus
Christ to the Youth of Tanzania,
East Africa

The Adventures of a
Maryknoll Priest
in Africa

Young Christian Students meet to discuss a youth retreat
during Holy Week

Book 2

Taken from Letters to my Mom

Father Marvin Deutsch M.M.

A Missionary's letters from Africa
1981 – 1997

Table of Contents

The Adventures of a Maryknoll Priest in Africa

Bringing the Good News of Jesus Christ to the Youth of Tanzania, East Africa

This book contains the personal history of Fr. Marvin Deutsch, M.M. ordained in 1957, by the Maryknoll Fathers Mission Society. He worked 33 years in Tanzania, E. Africa. This book is based on the many letters (about a thousand), written to his mother and other family members and friends.

Fr. Deutsch was following his God-given calling to go into the whole world and teach the gospel to every creature. (see Mark 16:15)

The Adventures of a Maryknoll Priest in Africa

Letters from Africa - Book 2

Chapter I

A Fantastic Year of Studies in Rome

The year was 1981. My work in Dar es Salaam had come to a close. I had received a new assignment as Secondary School Chaplain in Shinyanga Diocese, Tanzania. I was 53 years old, had been ordained 24 years, was given a sabbatical, and decided to take higher studies in Rome for one school year.

There were various reasons for going to Rome for studies and not some place else. In my mind, we were all suffering from change. Some of the changes were very good, but some changes seemed to bring confusion and misdirection. I was not satisfied with many of the theological interpretations that were coming from the Vatican Council. I felt that our faith was often being watered down, for example, that conversion to Christ and entrance into the Church, was no longer necessary. I considered these aberrations and misinterpretations of the Council. I felt this very strongly but did not know enough to refute them. I wanted an opportunity to read the documents myself. Also, Rome is the center of the Roman Catholic Church. I wanted to be near that center and near the Pope, the principle of unity for all of Christendom. Also, I had heard from others who had studied in Rome, that the two universities, the Angelicum and the Gregorian, were receiving students like myself, who were not necessarily interested in a degree, but wanted upgrading and renewal. The tuition was not expensive, only several hundreds dollars a school year. We also had a very nice domicile in Rome within walking distance to the two universities. It all seemed every ideal. I couldn't wait to get there. A few Maryknollers gave me some advice. They said - just audit the courses (which meant you would not have to take the exams, but at the same time would receive no credit.) They said you are too old and undisciplined to tackle all those studies and keep up with the young seminarians who were taking the courses. I did not accept this advice and decided to take the plunge. I would take the courses for credit and tackle the exams. This turned out to be a very wise decision. I had no trouble keeping up with the younger people taking the courses and did very well in the exams. In fact, I ended up with a 93 average. In Rome, I kept up my custom of writing to my mother almost weekly. Thus I begin with my first letter:

Collegio Maryknoll
Via Sardegna 83
00187 Rome, Italy

Oct. 1, 1981

Dear Mom,

It is 6:30 P.M. which is 12:30 P.M. your time. I am writing this from the Rome Maryknoll house. I arrived here about 2 P.M. and already have all my bags unpacked and everything arranged in my room. I had a very good trip. I was very happy that Northwest checked my big bag all the way through. I didn't have to touch it again until I got to Rome.

While waiting for the Alitalia plane at Kennedy Airport (I had a 5 hour wait since the plane was delayed one hour) I met a priest from Buffalo, Fr. Bob Conlon, who was on my same flight to Rome. Fr. Bob just celebrated his 25th anniversary and his parish gave him a gift of a two week trip to Rome. Fr. Bob studied in Rome as a seminarian for 5 years and had not been back since his ordination 25 years ago. We had a good time together. It turned out that he knew several Maryknollers and went to high school with one of my classmates, Fr. Dennis Kraus. We sat together on the plane, a big 747. I asked for seats in front of one of the exits and so we had plenty of leg room and could stretch out. They served us a nice supper of steak and ravioli with a small bottle of wine. I slept 2 or 3 hours before the sun came up.

We got to Rome about 11 A.M. Rome time. Fr. Bob's friend, an Indian priest, Fr. Peter, was there to meet us. They were classmates 25 years ago. Fr. Peter now works in Rome and is in charge of tourism for the Church. After we picked up our baggage, he brought us to our places, Fr. Bob to his hotel, and me to Collegio Maryknoll. Waiting for the baggage was the only hitch in an otherwise very good trip. The baggage workers were on slow-down strike. We had to wait 2 hours before they finally unloaded the baggage. But I really didn't mind. I was just happy to see my bag on the conveyor belt. It was really easy. We even had a little cart, supplied by the airport to wheel the bag to the car.

When I got to the Maryknoll house, the maid showed me to my room. It is on the 4th (top) floor and is very nice.

The fourth floor is for priests and brothers going to school. The 2nd and third floors are for resident priests and guests. I liked the 4th floor better because it is quiet and the rooms are smaller and therefore warmer in the cool weather. The room is about 13' by 18' which is still a pretty good size. There is a sink in the room and shower and toilet right across the hall. I guess there will be 3 more up here so we will have a nice community. There is a stairway going up to the roof. You can sit up there on a nice day and there are also clothes lines for hanging out wash. I unpacked my little radio. It works very well. There are many stations in Rome.

After supper this evening (supper is at 7 P.M.) Fr. Charles Schlecht, a non Maryknoller who is a resident here, explained to me   how to call the U.S.   You can dial direct - just dial 001 and then the area code and number. I tried twice. The first time the line was busy. The second time I got through right away. The calls are not so expensive - I think about $5 for three minutes. The temperature was 72 degrees when we arrived at the airport. It is about the same in my room right now, 9:30 P.M.

I hope you got the furnace turned on without much delay. I think it is good that Margaret and John went home. A week and a half is long enough. Life here should not be so different from the U.S. It should be a good year. I feel pretty good, not too tired, but I think I will go to bed early and start fresh tomorrow.

Hi to all from Rome..... Love,
Fr. Marv

The above is a postcard I sent my mother.

Last Sunday I visited one of the big museums where the statue of this she-wolf is housed. The two little children are Remus and Remulus. They are, according to the legend, the offspring of a woman, Rea Silva and the God Mars. The children were abandoned on the shores of the Tiber River which runs through Rome, and were suckled by the she-wolf. When the children grew up, they became the founders of Rome in 753 B.C.

(Describes the belief in Rome's false gods)

Rome

Friday, Oct. 9, 1981

Dear Mom,

I have been in Rome now just a little over a week. Yesterday I finished registration. That took several days of filling out forms, getting the proper approvals and paying for the tuition. I have a good schedule of classes. I am taking four subjects at the Angelicum (University run by the Dominicans) and one subject at the Gregorian (university run by the Jesuits). The two universities are not far apart, just a few blocks. I can easily walk from the Maryknoll house to either one of them in about 25 minutes; or I can take a bus which takes just about the same amount of time. School starts on October 16th.

The weather has really been nice. The temperature today is about 75 degrees. It goes down to about 65 degrees at night which is just about ideal.

The Vatican has its own radio station which gives us all the news of the Church, speeches of the Pope, news of the world, etc. The broadcasts are in many languages. Twice a day they are in English. On Wednesday, the pope had his first audience in St. Peter's Square. since he was shot last May 13th. I didn't go but listened to his talk on the radio.

The shooting of President Sadat of Egypt was a terrible thing. The pope in his speech on Wednesday praised Sadat for all he had done for peace and offered prayers and condolences for his wife and family. No Arab has been as well liked by Christians and Jews as has been Sadat. It is a great loss to the world.

There are 4 of us living here at the house who will be taking special studies, Fr. Joe Slaby, Fr. Joe Lafort (a 61 year old   priest from Calgary, Canada), Brother John Beeching, and myself. We have a nice community. Brother Phillip who is 84 years old, takes care of the house and does the shopping. He has been here about 25 years.

Till next week - much love and prayers,
Fr. Marv

Rome

Oct. 19, 1981

Dear Mom,

Many thanks for your letter of Oct. 9 which arrived today. That took 10 days so I see the mail coming here takes just about as long as the mail going to Africa.

Yesterday, Sunday, I went for a bike ride with Brother Andy Marsolek. There is one bike which belongs to the house. We rented another at the park which is just a couple of blocks away and spent about 2 hours cruising around. It was great fun. There is very little traffic on Sunday morning. We visited the Olympic stadiums and the Piazza del Populo. There are so many things to see in Rome, and going by bicycle is much faster, of course, than walking.

I am enjoying my classes. It is not difficult for me to get back to the books because I have been doing quite a bit of studying right along. I am happy I spent the time at home studying Italian. I am not fluent, but I know enough to get around and can ask questions. The help in the house does not speak English and so I get a chance to practice with them.

Yesterday, Sunday afternoon, I attended a Charismatic prayer meeting at the Gregorian University from 4 to 6 P.M. There were two guest speakers, Cardinal Suenens from Belgium and Sr. Bridgett from Ireland. They both spoke on the healing ministry. Sr. Bridgett is quite famous as a healer. Through her prayers many people have been cured of their illnesses. She travels all around the world speaking, praying and healing.

The weather has been very mild. I wear a sweater, but in the afternoon short sleeves are comfortable. Greetings to Jack, Don, Marlys, Dorothy and all. Tell them I am enjoying Rome.

Till next week, much love,
Fr. Marv

Footnote:

Brother Andy Marsolek is a Maryknoll brother. In the fall of 1981 he was taking a renewal course at the SVD renewal center in Nemi, about 30 miles from Rome. He often came to the Maryknoll house on weekends.

Felice Compleanno *(Happy Birthday in Italian)*

Rome

Oct. 23, 1981

Dear Mom,

Thanks for your letter of Oct. 19th. All is fine here. It has been raining off and on the past couple of days, but they say that this is usual for late Oct. and November.

This evening the pope had a 6 P.M. mass for all the students and teachers in Rome at St. Peter's. We were all there. It was wonderful. Thousands of People attended. The mass and sermon were in Italian.

My special prayers and mass for you on your birthday.
Much love, always,
Fr. Marv

Footnote:

I had an interesting experience about this time in Rome. I was on the bus, not seated, but standing and holding on to the strap. I was surprised to see the person standing next to me was the Salvatorian, Brother Andy whom I knew very well in Dar es Salaam. I asked him what he was doing in Rome. He said he was just stopping over and was on his way to his home in Wisconsin. He asked me what I was doing here. I said that I was taking a year off for studies. He asked me what I was studying. I mentioned the courses which included the Thomistic notion of the Seven Capital Sins. To my surprise, Brother Andy burst out laughing. I asked him what he was laughing about. "Oh", he said, "sin is passé now. We don't worry about that anymore."

I guess I should not have been surprised at his answer. That was the very reason I had come to Rome to study. The lack of the importance of sin was one of the misinterpretations of the Vatican Council. In fact, Pope John Paul said quite frequently that the greatest problem of our times is the loss of the sense of sin.

St. Peter's Basilica as seen at night from across the Tiber

Rome

Christmas Day, 1981

Dear Mom,

Received your letter of Dec. 3 on Dec. 22. I offered mass for Larry Wallace yesterday. In a way, he was very fortunate to have the opportunity to prepare for death. I would have wished that for Rose too. But they are both now in the hands of the merciful Lord.

We had a very nice Christmas here. Some of the Fathers went to the midnight mass at St. Peter's last night. I am not so fond of staying up so late, so I went to bed early and said the mass at dawn with Brother Philip attending. We had a community concelebrated mass at 10 A.M. after which we watched a beautiful television broadcast of Christmas singing. At 12 noon the pope was televised from the balcony of St. Peter's where he gave his Christmas message to the thousands of people in St. Peter's square. The pope, after his Christmas speech which was in Italian, gave Christmas greetings in over 20 languages. He even gave one in Kiswahili which of course I picked out right away. At 1 P.M. we had an elegant Christmas dinner - ham, sweet potatoes, peas, wine, and even Champaign.

Tomorrow Fr. Joe Laforte and I will take the bus to the SVD seminary at Nemi, which is about 20 miles from the city of Rome, where we will spend 6 days on retreat. We expect to be back here at the Maryknoll house on New Year's Eve.

I want to wish you a very happy New Year - "Un Buon Anno" in Italian. I'll be calling you on either January 1 or 2. I am very happy to hear that Dorothy is doing well.

> *Love and prayers,*
> *Fr. Marv.*

Footnote:

My sister, Rose was married to Larry Wallace who was divorced. Rose died first suddenly of a heart attack. Larry died shortly after but was reconciled with the Church before he died.

The Christmas dinner, 1981

Left to right:
Sitting: Brother Philip, Fr. Joe O'Neil (superior) a guest Bishop whose name I don't remember, Brother Andy Marsolek and Brother John Beeching
Standing: Our cook, Fr. Vince Mallon, Fr. Marvin Deutsch, a guest priest, and Fr. Joe Slaby

Footnote:

Fr. Joe Laforte and I enjoyed our retreat at Nemi run by the Society of the Divine Word Priests and brothers (SVD). It was a private and directed retreat which means that you don't have lectures, but the retreat master gives you scripture passages to read and meditate upon. He meets with you twice a day to discuss with you what you have been praying and thinking about in responding to the scripture passages. This was my first directed retreat. It was important for me because of my intention to learn how to give this kind of a retreat to others. When the new school semester was to begin I had planned to take the course on Ignatian retreat methods at the Gregorian university. This retreat was a good preparation for this course.

Nemi Renewal Center - Run by the SVD Fathers

View of the Volcanic Lake from the center - Fr. Joe Laforte took my picture there.

Rome

January 11, 1982

Dear Friends,

In this letter I would like to tell you about some of my "explorations" during my free time here in Rome. One of the reasons
I like being here is the sense of reality it gives one with the past. You can touch with your hands ancient ruins which existed at the time of the Apostles and affected their lives.

Last Sunday, Fr. Joe Laforte and I walked around the ancient Roman Forum which runs along the base of the Palatine hill. It is about a 40 minute walk from our house. The Palatine hill is one of the 7 hills of Rome and the one upon which Rome is said to have been founded in the year 754 B.C. Today on this hill you can still see the ruins of the palaces of the Caesars. Augustus, who was Roman emperor at the time when Jesus was born, lived here. Walking along the forum (the seat of government), you can see the ruins of the house of the Roman senate, pagan temples and other memorials. We walked through the white marble arch of Titus, which was built to commemorate the victory of Titus over the Jews when he destroyed the city and temple of Jerusalem in the year 70 A.D. Engravings on the arch depict a procession of Roman soldiers carrying the 7 branch candlestick and other vessels they had looted from the temple. Figures of Jews can be seen chained as they walk surrounded by Roman soldiers.

At the end of the forum we visited the prison where Saints Peter and Paul were supposedly held before they were martyred around the year 67 A.D. The prison which is more like an underground dungeon, is the oldest intact structure in Rome. It goes back to 300 B.C. Today there is a church built over the dungeon. You can walk down a flight of stairs into the dungeon which is built completely of stone, and no doubt, the reason it has survived all these years. The dungeon must have been a terrible place to be since it is below ground, has no windows and is damp and dreary inside.

On another day we walked to the catacombs of St. Priscilla, about a 40 minute walk in another direction from our house. As you may know, the catacombs are meandering tunnels where the early Christians buried their dead, held meetings and liturgical functions during the persecutions in the first 3 centuries. There are many catacombs, but the one named after ST. Priscilla is especially interesting. When it was dug by the Christians (begun at the beginning of the second century and expanded over the next 2 to 3 hundred years) it was outside the walls of old Rome. Today it is right under a section of the city and goes in various directions for a total distance of 3 miles. There are paintings on the walls in crypt-like areas which were little chapels. One painting which you can still make out is of the Madonna and child, and is the earliest in picture of the existence of Mary, going back to about the year 125 A.D. There are other pictures of the Good Shepherd, also Abraham offering his son, Isaac, illustrating the faith and devotion of the early Christians. A little old sister, dressed in a ski-jacket over her black habit, showed us around through the dimly lit tunnels. She said the bones of the martyrs were carried off by vandals in the many sackings of Rome in the early centuries, who brought them to their own countries for superstitious reasons. However, the empty niches where they were buried are still there.

The first semester will be finished at the end of January. Then come final exams. Next semester I will be doing a lot of studies in Church History which should be interesting and exciting.....The weather conditions continue to be mild with temperatures usually in the 50's. I would' like to close this letter with a blessing taken from the book of Numbers (6:23) which the venerable old Dominican, Fr. Duncker (82 years old), who teaches us Scripture at the Angelicum, uses to open each class.

The Lord bless you and keep you. The Lord let his face shine upon you, and be gracious to you. The Lord look upon you kindly and give you peace.

Love and peace,
Fr. Marv

Rome

Jan. 18, 1982

Dear Mom,

Many thanks for your letter of Jan. 5 which arrived a few days ago. Dorothy's letter with the pictures enclosed arrived at the same time as yours although it was written one month earlier. I think all the Christmas mail has caught up now.

Sounds like you are having very cold weather with quite a bit of snow, but I guess that is to be expected this time of year. Here the weather continues to be mild - in the 50's. It is quite a bit warmer than I expected for January.

Last Sunday, Fr. Joe Laforte, Brother John Beeching, and myself, continued our exploration. We visited the ruins of the baths of Diocletian. The baths were built around the year 175 A.D. and were
a huge series of buildings covering a whole city block. It included a huge gymnasium with adjoining baths and steam rooms. Part of the building was turned into a church in the year 1575, called the Church of Our Lady of the Angels, which

is still used today. In fact, mass was going on when we walked in. The church is about twice the size of St. Helena's which gives you some idea how they built things in those days. The church was only a small part of the original baths.

I am busy reviewing and preparing for exams which will be coming up at the end of the month. Classes are still going on, of course. I got news a few days ago that Fr. Dan Ohmann's mother was killed in a car accident about 2 or 3 weeks ago. You may remember I drove up with the other Maryknollers to Freeport (MN) last summer to attend the funeral of Dan's father.

All is fine here. I hope you are not suffering too much from the cold and that your house is nice and warm. My regards to everyone. Say hello to your neighbor, Norrie Fry, too. I am glad to hear that she helps you out once in a while.

> Much love and daily prayers,
> Fr. Marv

P.S. Tell Marlys the shoes she got me for my birthday are really getting a workout and holding up beautifully.

Rome

Tuesday, Jan. 26, 1982

Dear Mom,

I see in the Herald Tribune that you had quite a storm in Minneapolis over the weekend. The story was on the front page and had a picture of a car half buried by the snow. The article said you had 40 inches. That sounds something like the Armistice Day blizzard on Nov. 11 when we were kids. I wonder how the roof on the new domed stadium is holding up. I heard that it collapsed under the weight of snow in December. Here the weather continues to be mild. Those who were here last year said that January was much cooler and rainy, and so I guess I hit a good time to come here.

I had my last class of the first semester today. I have 4 exams to take, but the first one is not until a week from now, so I have quite a bit of time to review and prepare.

Last Wednesday Fr. Joe Laforte and I went to the opera, "Tosca", which was very interesting. The opera house is very old, yet very beautiful on the inside. It was redecorated in 1928 during the reign of Mussolini. There is a plaque over the stage that has his name on it. Opera is very popular among the Italians. The house was full. The audience show their appreciation by shouting "Bravo, Bravo" after a good solo by one of the singers. I think I enjoyed the audience as much as the show.

Tomorrow night, Fr. Joe and I are going to the Beda College to play cards. The Beda is a special seminary for belated vocations, older men who want to become priests. Thomas Murphy, a former lawyer in the U.S. and about 45 years old, is the one who invited us over. Seems like there are many vocations among middle aged men.

I just got Marlys' Christmas card on Jan. 21. I see it is postmarked Dec. 7. I think that took the longest of any mail that I have received. I received Don's letter saying that he had contacted the secretary at St. Helena's parish, Eloise, confirming June 20th for my mass and reception celebrating my 25 anniversary to the priesthood. I had forgotten about the need to reserve Rowan Hall. That will work out real well for the reception..... I hope you are not trying to shovel the snow. It is too heavy. Let someone else do it...

Till next week...Love and prayers

Fr. Marv

Rome

Feb. 4, 1982

Dear Mom,

Yesterday I had my final exam on the epistles and teaching of St. Paul, so now I can relax a little. I think I did well. The course was a very good one. I learned so much. It took a great deal of preparation and was very worthwhile. I now understand St. Paul. I still have 3 exams left, but they will be oral and short.

The big news on T.V. here and in the newspapers was the rescue of the American, General Dozier from the terrorist group, the Red Brigades, who had kidnapped him last December. The Italian police did a wonderful job in tracking down the hideout which was an apartment over a supermarket in the city of Padua. Perhaps you saw something on T.V about this.

I have found someone to play tennis with, Tom Murphy, the former American lawyer who is studying for the priesthood at the Beda seminary here in Rome. We will play next week when my exams are finished.

I hope this finds you well and the weather getting warmer. The weather continues to be lovely here - sunny and in the 50's.

Till next week, love and prayers,

Fr. Marv

Footnote:

One of the reasons I wanted to go to Rome to study was to find a good course on the teachings of St. Paul. For hundreds of years there have been conflicts about his teachings, especially when he wrote about salvation - whether it comes from faith or good works. Martin Luther said it comes from Faith. Good work has nothing to do with it. What I discovered in the excellent course I had, taught by Dr. Parsons at the Angelicum (Dominican priest) was that St. Paul taught that justification (conversion and reconciliation with God) comes through the grace of Jesus Christ who died on the cross for us so that our sins could be forgiven and we could be reconciled with God. In order to receive this grace one needs to repent and believe. So faith is important, but it must be accompanied with sorrow for sin and the purpose of amendment, something the Catholic Church had always taught and which makes perfect sense. St. Paul was not teaching that good works have no meaning regarding salvation. What he was teaching was that the old law with all of its customs like circumcision and the like, cannot redeem us, take away our sins and reconcile us with God. Only Christ can. As regards salvation, reconciliation with God is not sufficient. We must continue to be faithful to God by love and good works after being reconciled. In other words, we must die in the state of grace in order to be saved and enter into the kingdom of God. Justification is the first step; salvation is the last.

Rome

Feb. 15, 1982, Monday

Dear Mom,

It was real good to talk to you on the phone yesterday. You sound fine. We started the new semester today. I had two classes at the Angelicum , one, a course on counseling and one on Church history.

On Tuesday I have a repeat of Monday. On Wednesday I have two periods at the Gregorian, one on the letter to the Hebrews, taught by Fr. Barnabas Ahern, and the second one on Spiritual direction, taught by an Indian Jesuit, Fr. Alphonso. On Saturday I am back at the Angelicum for a class on the Vatican Council document, Dei Verbum (The dogmatic Constitution on Divine Revelation), taught by Fr. Dunker, the Dutch Dominican. It is not a real heavy schedule, but enough for it gives me a chance to do outside study. I want to read all the Vatican Council documents before leaving Rome.

Last Sunday, (the day I called)) I went to the Russian Catholic Eastern rite church just to see how they do it. They have beautiful singing, but I don't care too much for their liturgy. There is no community participation. Everything is done by the priests in the sanctuary which during the most important part of the mass - the consecration - is closed off by a curtain. During that precious time, no one can see what is going on there. I think they should change some of the old practices to let the laity in on what is going on. I guess the Easter rites were not affected much by the Vatican Council.

The weather continues to be mild. It must have been close to 60 today.

Much love and daily prayers...
Fr. Marv

P.S. *Please tell Dorothy I said mass for Wally on Feb. 7.*

Footnote:

Wally was my sister Dorothy's husband who had died in 1961 age 43.

Rome

Feb. 25, 1982

Dear Mom,

Many thanks for your letter of Feb. 16 which took only about one week to come. It is quite amazing to hear about all the snow you have had. There is going to be a lot of water around when it all starts to melt.

We have finished the first week of the new semester and are off to a flying start. It doesn't take long to have a lot of work to do, but it is all very interesting. They say that History repeats itself. So many of the present problems and attitudes are similar to the period around Martin Luther's time. Present day thinking cannot be understood without reference to the past. The pendulum swings back and forth from one extreme to the other and rarely stops in the center.

Today is the second day in Lent. The pope had a mass yesterday,
Ash Wednesday, at San Sabina church which is one of the oldest in Rome. Only a limited number of people could attend, but it was televised so we could all watch. The pope looks good, even after his exhausting trip to West Africa.

Our weather has been a little bit cooler, but still nice. It is in the 50's today.
My love and greetings to all... Happy Lent.
Fr. Marv.

Rome

March 1982

SPRING EASTER LETTER
Peace is to enjoy a sunset and know who to thank.

Dear Friends,

One of the joys of my study leave here in Rome has been the opportunity to explore various parts of this great city to better understand important events which took place in the past. Down through the ages saints and sinners have walked down the streets of Rome leaving their mark on history.

Recently I visited the Aventine Hill, one of the 7 hills upon which Rome was founded. At the top of the hill there is a church called Santa Sabina which was built in the 5th Century over the ruins of a pagan temple. About the year 1220, the church was given to St. Dominic by Pope Honorius III and thus became the headquarters for the newly founded congregation of the Dominicans. Dominic added a cloister for his monks and it was here that the Blessed Virgin Mary appeared to him asking him to promote the rosary. In the courtyard today one can see an orange tree which some say was planted by St. Dominic. Others say that the original tree died and the present one is a mere 300 years old. Whatever, it sure looks old. It is all craggy and knotted. St. Dominic brought the orange tree from his home in Spain because in those days there were no orange trees in Rome. Anyhow, the other day when I was there, there was an orange hanging on it, and this is not the season for oranges. Upon entering the church, one is struck by the beauty of a large wooden door upon which are carved scenes of the bible. This door, carved in the 5th century, is credited to be the oldest carved wooden door in the world.

A short distance from Santa Sabina is the beautiful monastery of Santa Anselm, built by the Benedictines about the year 1900. Visitors are welcome here to attend mass on Sunday where Gregorian chant is sung by the monks in a most perfect way. When I was there they were getting ready for a wedding. Workers in a few minutes unrolled a huge red rug which was mounted on a metal circular rack, a clever device no doubt invented by the German element in the community.

For those specially devoted to St. Ignatius, the founder of the Jesuits, one can visit the church of the Gesu (Jesus) located near the Piazza Venezia, built shortly after the death of St. Ignatius. (Ignatius died in the year 1556; the church was begun in 1568). The church is very black on the outside from all the pollution of buses and cars that pass by, but on the inside it is very beautiful, one of the first of the baroque style, which became so popular in church architecture throughout Europe in the 17th C. But more important, this church marks the spot where St. Ignatius prayed. Before this church was built, a small church was there called Santa Maria della Strada (St. Mary of the Street). St. Ignatius had his humble apartments next store where he spent the last 15 years of his life running his newly founded society which numbered a thousand members at his death and so effectively stemmed the tide of the Lutheran rebellion and brought the Church back to striving for holiness. Today the body of St. Ignatius lies beneath a side altar. On the opposite side is enshrined the arm of St. Francis Xavier. Francis, who was from Spain, was one of the first members of the Jesuits and probably would have succeeded Ignatius had he not died a premature death as a missionary on Sancien Island off the coast of China.

About a 5 minute walk from the Gesu, one can visit the 13th C church, Santa Maria sopra Minerva. The word "sopra" in Italian means "above". Hence the name. The church of St. Mary was built over the pagan temple dedicated to the Roman Goddess, Minerva. This church has the body of St. Catherine of Siena enshrined in a glass case beneath the main altar. St. Catherine is best known for convincing Pope Gregory XI, who was living in Avignon, France, to return to Rome in the year 1377. Later Catherine came to Rome from Siena and died here very close to the church, Santa Maria Sopra Minerva, where she lived with other Dominican sisters.

There are over 450 major churches in Rome, each with its fascinating history recalling the struggle of good and evil in the past. But Rome is not dead. It is very much alive. There is usually a crowd of at least 50,000 people each Sunday in St. Peter's square to listen to the 12 noon message of Pope John Paul II, and many times that on big feast days.

I see my space is running out and so I will close this letter wishing you Easter joy. I pray for each of you and your intentions every morning at mass. During this season our hearts are filled with hope, especially as we think about the promise of Jesus which has so much meaning for each one of us. For the time will come when he will "transform these imperfect bodies of ours into copies of his glorious body" (Phil 3:21). Happy feast day of the resurrection!

Peace in the risen lord,
Fr. Marvin Deutsch

Rome

March 14, 1982

Dear Mom,

Last Thursday Fr. Joe Slaby and I went to help the sisters of Mother Theresa who have a house of charity near the railway station. They work with the outcasts of society, the bums and alcoholics who are homeless and hang around the railway station. The sisters have a clean place in the basement of a building and are well organized, giving about 35 men a good supper and a place to sleep for the night. The little brothers who were also organized by Mother Theresa, came before supper to give a half hour prayer service. Everyone participated including a few bums who were quite drunk and made quite a bit of noise at the wrong time. Fr. Joe and I helped in the preparation of the supper and cleaning up afterwards. I am quite impressed with the work of the sisters. Christ still walks among the poor.

Today for lunch I was invited to the Casa Maria which is the residence for the American priests who are taking the special 3 month renewal program for priests here in Rome. There are about 90 priests of all ages from all over the U.S. I met one priest from Canon Falls, New Ulm diocese, Fr. Jim Moran. The Casa Maria has a magnificent chapel built around the year 1700 at a time when it was a sisters' convent.

About a hundred years later when Napoleon invaded Rome, the beautiful building was used as a stable, a place to keep the army's horses. The Casa Maria is very close to Trevi Fountain. Also, the Gregorian University is only a short distance away. Rome is a fascinating place to visit and just full of history.

Happy Springtime, coming up soon,
Love and prayers,
Fr. Marv

Monday, March 22, 1982

Dear Mom,

Yesterday several of us Maryknollers participated in the mass at St. Peter's, said by the Holy Father for China. We were in the procession and helped with Holy Communion. I was very close to Pope John Paul. It was a moving experience.

Now that the door is opening a little in China, there remains a big problem - The Nationalist Catholic Church set up by the government in about 1952 is not in union with Rome. There seems to be no desire of this Church to want anything to do with Rome. The pope yesterday prayed for unity, "one faith, one Baptism, one Lord". He asked our Blessed mother to intercede that the Chinese Church may once again be united to the Chair of Peter. The pope spoke in Italian. I could understand some of it since he speaks slowly.

I hope this finds you feeling well and getting some nice Spring weather. All is fine with me... Happy Springtime,
Love,
Fr. Marv

St. Peter's Basilica

April 3, 1981

Dear Mom,

I want to thank you for your two letters of March 10 and March 23. Both arrived on the same day. I am happy to hear you have no snow damage to the roof. That was very nice of your neighbor Nora, to have her husband help you to clean the snow off of your roof. Give them my greetings.

This morning I had my last class before the Easter break. We have two weeks off from school which seems like a long time. I have a long term paper to write so this will be a good time to do it. Then, of course, to be here for Holy Week will be a great joy. Also, there is a woman, Michaelina McCloughlan whom I knew some years ago in Dar es Salaam, who is coming to Rome for a visit. She works for the Canadian Embassy and is now stationed in Beirut, Lebanon. Brother John Beeching, who is studying Arabic here in Rome and occupies the room across the hall from me, was stationed in Beirut for one year, and knows Michaelina well. So does Sr. Ursula. It will be nice to plan a few things together while Michaelina is here.

Happy Easter, Mom. Greetings to all...
Love, Fr. Marv

April 14, 1982

Dear Mom,

I haven't received any Easter mail yet, but no doubt that is due to the Italian Easter Holidays. Everything closes down for about 4 days here in Rome over Easter.

I enjoyed the Holy Week ceremonies very much. On Holy Thursday morning all the priests of Rome were invited to St. Peter's with the Holy Father. There were 1500 priests present. It was quite impressive to experience the oneness of the priesthood with the Pope.

On Good Friday, I attended the ceremony at St. Anselms which is the Benedictine headquarters for the whole world. The ceremony was in Latin and Italian, and the singing was very well done by the monks.

For the Easter Vigil service all of us Maryknollers went to San Susana church which is run by the Paulist Fathers for the Americans in Rome. The service was in English and I think the first time for me to be able to participate in a Holy Week service in my own language.

The most impressive of all was Easter Sunday. The mass was held outside St. Peter's in the huge square. This was the biggest crowd of people I have ever seen - 300,000 people according to the estimate in the newspaper. There were people from all over the world. The Swiss Guard, protectors of the pope, came marching into the square and stood at attention in the middle of the square for the entire mass. There were two military bands, one on either side of the Swiss Guard, that added to the festive joy of the occasion. It was a real experience of Christian unity under the pope, all professing faith in the risen Christ, the Lord of all creation.

There are no classes this week. We begin again on Monday. There are just 6 weeks left of school. The time is going quickly.... I hope you finally have some warm weather.

Much love,

Fr. Marv

Footnote:

There was an incident that happened on Good Friday that I did not write about in my letters. Four of us Maryknollers attended the ceremony at 3 P.M. at San Anselm. After the ceremony was over we decided to walk along the Tiber River and stop in at the Church of San Sabina which was perhaps three quarters of a mile away. As we were walking along the Tiber we noticed a path going almost straight up to the great height where the Church of San Sabina was built. The path wound its way through bushes and rocks to the top perhaps about 75 yards away. We decided to ascend up this path which would save us a half mile of walking. When we were close to the top we noticed some caves. They appeared empty but amazingly enough, there were some syringes laying on ground outside the caves. We proceeded to another cave and were surprised to see a bearded youth sitting in front of the cave and staring out into space. He seemed out of it and totally unaware of our presence; or, if he did see us, he made no sign of recognition. We realized, of course, that he was high on drugs and probably had just shot himself up. We had heard that there are many youth in Rome who live this strange life of drug addiction. There are certain places where they periodically meet.

The above picture was taken on Holy Thursday when we priests (1500) concelebrated the Holy Chrism mass with Pope John Paul II. I am there someplace in the foreground.

There are many fountains in Rome. The top picture is the Trevi fountain, made famous by the film, "Three Coins in the Fountain". It is an old custom to throw coins into this fountain and make a wish. I go by the Trevi fountain often. It is near the Gregorian University.

Rome

April 26, 1982

Dear Mom,

Seems like it has been a couple of weeks since I have heard from anyone, but I did get a letter from Sr. Leonarda for Easter. I hope everything is o.k.   We have had damp, rather cold and rainy weather this past week. With all the nice weather we had in January, February and March, I guess we can expect some nasty weather too.

A week ago Sunday I visited the Good Shepherd sisters' mother house, which is on the other side of town. Fr. Charles Schleck, a Holy Cross Father who lives with us, hears confessions there on Sundays, so I rode over with him. Sister Mary Eudes, who is from St. Paul, had invited me for dinner. She is a good friend of Sr. Mary (Lawrence) Stoffel of the same order. Sr. Mary Eudes is an older sister and has been asked to be their cook at their Rome house for a couple of years. She seems to like it here very much.

I am planning my trip back to the U.S. and will arrange for my ticket this week. As I see it now, I will leave here on June 3rd and arrive in Minneapolis the evening of the same day. I will be able to stay in Minneapolis until about June 24, which is almost 3 weeks, before going to Maryknoll, N.Y. to celebrate my 25th anniversary with my classmates. I

---

expect to be back in Tanzania on July 1. To have the opportunity to be at home for a few weeks is a gift from the Lord.

Greetings to all the family. I am looking forward to seeing everybody.

Prayers and much love,
Fr. Marv

Rome

May 2, 1982
Happy Mother's Day

Dear Mom,

I hope this arrives in time for Mothers' Day. I will remember you very especially at mass where we are all together in the Lord.

Today was a fun day. Brother Phillip, the 84 year old (young) Maryknoller who has been working at our house in Rome for the past 25 years, and I, went to his niece's home in the small town of Agnani for the weekend. Agnani is a very ancient town built in the foothills of a small mountain about 30 miles Southeast of Rome. This little town has the unique distinction of being the birthplace of 3 popes. It also has the distinction of being the birthplace of Brother Phillip. Brother Phillip came to America with his parents when he was 7 years old. Since the family spoke Italian at home, he never forgot his native language. Brother showed us the house where he was born and the church of St. Andrew's where he was baptized. The church was built in the 13th Century, which gives you some idea of how old this town is. The streets of the town are very narrow since they were built for donkey carts. The ancient buildings are made of stone. Today, with so many cars, the streets are all "one way" for the simple reason they are too narrow for 2 cars to pass. Today there was a bicycle race up and down the hilly streets, which added to the excitement. From the open spaces in the town, you can see the surrounding valleys where sheep are grazing and pastures are green with spring time.

We drove back to Rome about 6 P.M. The grapevines are just beginning to sprout leaves and the little farms looked beautiful. It was a pleasant experience and gave me a better idea of the Italian countryside, enriching my experience in this sabbatical year.

I hope this finds all well with you and that you had a wonderful Mother's Day.

Love,

Fr. Marv

Footnote:

This letter brings to a close my Sabbatical in Rome. There are no more letters saved by my mother coming from Rome. I finished my exams in early June and went back to the U.S. to celebrate my 25th anniversary as a priest. I fulfilled all my wishes that I had hoped for in Rome. (see first page of this book)

I had an excellent course on St. Paul, taught by Dr. (Fr) Parsons. I not only read all the Vat. II documents, but also had a course on the Dogmatic Constitution of Divine Revelation, by Fr.Duncker which defines revelation as the source of all our knowledge of God and also is the fundamental source of our Catholic Faith. The course I had on the 7 Capital sins at the Angelicum University was an excellent backdrop for the course I had on Ignatian retreat methods and another on Spiritual Direction at the Gregorian. After these courses I felt qualified to be a retreat master and spiritual director in the future.

Footnote:

After finishing my exams, I left Rome for Minneapolis where I celebrated my 25th anniversary as a priest. My aunt, Sr. Leonarda, helped me prepare a collage using pictures of my ordination in 1957 and various pictures from my work in Africa. I celebrated mass at my home parish of St. Helena's, and had a reception later in the parish hall. I also went to Maryknoll, N.Y. to celebrate with my classmates. By July, I was on my way and soon back in Dar es Salaam as the next letter of July 5 will indicate.

JUNE 17, 1982

Fr. Deutsch to note 25th anniversary

The Rev. Marvin F. Deutsch, MM, will celebrate the 25th anniversary of his ordination as a Maryknoll priest at his home parish, St. Helena's, Minneapolis, Sunday.

Fr. Deutsch

After a con-celebrated Mass at noon, he will greet friends at a reception in the parish hall until 3 p.m.

Fr. Deutsch was ordained June 8, 1957, at Maryknoll, NY. He worked in Tanzania from 1957 to 1963 and was superior of the Maryknoll house in Minneapolis from 1964 to 1969, when he returned to Tanzania to do pastoral and youth work in Dar es Salaam until 1981.

During the past year, he has been on a sabbatical in Rome. After his anniversary celebration, he will return to Tanzania as a youth chaplain for the Diocese of Shinyanga.

JUNE 17, 1982

News digest

President and Mrs. Reagan and Pope John Paul II greet American seminarians at the Vatican after the two world leaders exchanged statements on world peace. The president said he had been visiting Europe on a "pilgrimage of peace."

The picture above appeared in the Catholic Bulletin, the St. Paul diocesan Catholic Newspaper, on June 17th 1982. It appeared in the same issue as my 25th anniversary article. It is interesting to note who was Pope and who was president of the United States at that time. Pope John Paul was 62 years old at that time.

Anniversary celebrations at Maryknoll, N.Y. - June 1982. My class of 1957 was celebrating our 25th. Others were celebrating their 40th, 50th, and 60th. I am the one on the right, top row. Fr. James Noonan (front row, 3rd from the left), was the Superior General at that time.

Chapter II

1982 - 6 Years as Chaplain at Shinyanga Secondary School

Dar es Salaam, Tanzania

Monday, July 5, 1982

Dear Mom,

I wanted to call you yesterday, but the phone here at the Dar house is temporarily out of order. The Lord has really helped me all the way. When I was checking my bags at the Rome airport, the check-in attendant wanted to charge me $300 for excess weight, but there was a Precious Blood priest going to Tanzania with 13 lay people (to build a hospital) who was right behind me in the line. He took me as his 14th person so my bags were weighed in with his group. Thus I paid nothing. The attendant was not too happy about it, but there was nothing he could do to make some extra cash. Also I had no problem with customs when I arrived at Dar es Salaam. I was very surprised. Having all that baggage, I didn't have to open a single one. Fr. John Lange was there to meet me in the wee hours of the morning.

I have been getting things ready for the move to Shinyanga. John got me some flour, rice and sugar - enough to keep me going for at least 3 months. Yesterday I packed all my tools and other things around here. We plan to leave in my V.W. kombi tomorrow morning after mass. Fr. Bill Hofferman is going with us so there will be lots of company. I am going to take my dog, Raha, along. He is in real good shape.

Yesterday Fr. John Lange and I played tennis with two White Fathers at the Youth Center. I was happy to go there especially to see how the place looks after one year. I was surprised to see how much the trees and bushes I had planted had grown. The whole place looked beautiful. It did my heart good to see how well Father George Smith carried on there after my departure. Fr. George is home on leave now and so I didn't get a chance to see him.

I went to the American Embassy the first day of arrival to get my passport renewed. It just took about an hour. They did it right away because of the 4th of July celebration which is being celebrated today, Monday, the 5th. Usually one has to come back to pick it up.

I took some nice pictures at Maryknoll - both of my classmates and also of Mrs. Grant and family - also several other couples whom I had met in 1974 when I participated in the marriage-encounter weekend during the renewal program at Maryknoll. I sent the negatives to Sr. Leonarda and asked her to send you some prints. In Rome I was able to get the film developed in one day and so I have enough prints for myself.

I guess that brings you pretty much up to date. I will write again when I get to Shinyanga.....Greetings to all...

Love and prayers,
Fr. Marv

Shinyanga

July 9th, 1982

Dear Mom,

A few words to tell you that Fr. John Lange, Fr. Bill Hefferman and I made the 620 mile trip from Dar es Salaam to Shinyanga, safely. We left Dar on July 6, and stayed overnight half way at Dodoma with the diocesan priests. They have a very nice guest house and also a place to lock up the V.W. The last 300 miles was a bit rough since the road is dirt all the way. When we arrived in Shinyanga, the muffler which was already bad when we left Dar, was completely finished, just hanging on by a thread. We spent all day yesterday putting on a new muffler. Fortunately, I had a spare which I had bought a couple of years ago. The V.W. is all fixed up again and ready to go.

You will be happy to hear that most of my boxes are here. When Brother Cyril was in Musoma for retreat, he loaded up his truck with whatever he could take and brought back 20 of my boxes. There still are about 10 up there which will probably be brought down toward the end of July. Also, the small deep freeze which John Lange had ordered for me from Germany, is already here in Shinyanga. There is a big diocesan warehouse here where I can put my things.

This afternoon John Lange and I are going out to the Secondary School, 18 miles from here, to bring out the first load of my things. John will help me get things set up in my new assignment. The Bishop, Castor Sequa, was very happy to see me. Everything is working out very well so far. The Lord is constantly looking after me.

Oh Yes, I mentioned, I brought Raha along. He seems right at home here in Shinyanga and seems to be enjoying the dry cooler climate.... Give my greetings to all the family. I will write again when I get settled at the Secondary School.
Love and prayers,
Fr. Marv

Footnote:

A funny thing happened on the trip. We were stopped at a police check point. The police officer demanded that we open up the sliding side door in the Volks. We knew, of course, that he was going to demand that we give him something, perhaps some soap or another item that was hard to get in a country of so many shortages. When I pulled the door open, there was my big dog Raha, staring us in the face. The policeman shouted, "Close the door and move on." It was so funny because Raha is such a kind, gentle dog. He wouldn't hurt a flea. We couldn't stop laughing for about a half hour. Raha saved us from a bribe.

Shinyanga Secondary School

July 16, 1982

Dear Mom,
Thank you for your letter of June 29 which arrived yesterday. It took about 2 weeks which I think will be the

usual time. Albert Popehn's death was to be expected. I will offer mass for him tomorrow.

It was just a week ago today that John Lange and I arrived here at Shinyanga Secondary School. John has been with me the entire week helping to get things set up and do some repairs. We have accomplished a lot in one week. Many things needed fixing - the lamps, my bed, the shower, the stove, etc. John helped me bring things from Shinyanga town (about 20 miles away) which were stored in the diocesan warehouse. We even have the new deep freeze set up and working. John went over to the Mwadui Diamond Mines shopping center today and brought me about 12 pounds of meat. The diamond mine is about a half mile away. Fr. Charles, who is the chaplain at the mines, brought me 2 bottles of milk, a pound of butter and 2 loaves of bread. I also have rice, flour and sugar. So you see I am in pretty good shape. I have everything here which was sent over in the shipment that I brought to Wisconsin except for 10 boxes. Brother Cyril said he didn't have room in his pickup for everything. But I expect to have the last 10 boxes within a month when someone else goes up to Musoma.

The heat regulator for the oven was not working on the electric stove when I first arrived but that's fixed too. A craftsman from the diamond mines came over to help me. I tried my hand at baking bread and it turned out terrific. I also tried making pizza and that turned out good too. I talked to the headmaster about my teaching schedule. I will start teaching on Monday, July 18th. Most of the students are back from vacation. I will have a meeting with the altar boys tomorrow and with the student parish council on Sunday after mass.

Fr. Charles Callahan from the mines, stops in almost every day and so I don't feel alone. My dog Raha is doing fine. Fr. Bill Tokus' dog, a German Shepard, was here when I came. His house boy, Charles, whom I have taken over, fed the dog and took care of the house for the last 6 months during the absence of a priest. The house was neat and clean when Fr. John and I arrived. The two dogs don't get along very well, but I think they will get used to each other. The Tupperware really is terrific. I am using it all.

My best to Dorothy, Deb, Marlys, Jack, Don and all.
Love,
Fr. Marv

Footnote:
Shinyanga Secondary School was built in the late 60's with U.S. money. The reason it was built 20 miles from Shinyanga town was because in order to get electricity and water, it had to be built next to the Diamond Mines. The directors of the mine (British) agreed to help out the school in this way. The first chaplain there was Maryknoller, Fr. Bill Tokus. He had a house, library and Chapel on the edge of the campus. Fr. Bill was there for 14 years. He left 6 months before my arrival and so there was no chaplain for 6 months. He had an Alsatian German shepherd dog given to him by the diamond mines because of a break-in by

thieves. The dog was very temperamental - a little bit crazy. The school was all boys - Form 1 through 6 (4 years high school and 2 years Junior college) About half were catholic. It was my job to teach all the religion classes.

There were so many shortages in Tanzania in the early 80's. We were sending over containers full of foodstuffs, building materials, etc. Brother Regis of the Salvatorians took care of the shipping out of New Holstein, Wisconsin.

Shinyanga Secondary School

July 24, 1982

Dear Mom,

Last Monday, July 19th, I started teaching. I have classes every day except Saturday. The schedule is not completely worked out yet, but fortunately the teacher in charge of the scheduling is a young volunteer from England, Dave Ecklund, who is doing everything he can to give me good periods. (not the afternoon periods when students aren't fresh) There are two volunteers from England, Dave and a young woman named Ann. The rest of the staff is African.

I have been over to the diamond mines several times. On Thursday I played tennis there with John Lange and a couple of Africans who work at the mines. They have a nice court and a good net. They lack tennis balls which I can supply.

Please tell Dorothy that I received her letter with the pictures, which I enjoyed. I will be writing to her in a couple of days. I am preparing a list of things to send in the next box.... I am enjoying the work here. It is a very good setup. I am continuing with my cooking and baking experiments. I made noodles the other day following your method.
Much love,
Fr. Marv

Footnote:

In Tanzania, religion classes are part of the curriculum. However, often times the classes are relegated to afternoon periods which are difficult to teach. Everybody is tired and because religion is not a credit subject, it is not easy to keep the attention of the students. Dave Ecklund gave me mostly morning periods for which I was very grateful.

Making noodles like mother - My mom made noodles the old fashioned way, by mixing eggs with flour and rolling the mix out into thin sheets. The sheets are left to dry and then are cupped up into noodles.

Shinyanga Secondary School

August 2, 1982

Dear Mom,

This is Monday afternoon and a chance to slow down a bit. I have been here just a little over 3 weeks. A lot has been accomplished. On Sunday I have mass in our chapel for the students at 9 A.M. Yesterday we had a high mass which was very colorful. The altar boys have fancy garb which Fr. Bill Tokus had made for them. There is a small pump organ which several of the students know how to play. Also they use drums which make the liturgies very joyful - real celebrations. After mass I began the catechumenate for students who want to become Catholics. There are about 20.

On Sunday afternoon I did some baking - made 5 loaves of bread and also some noodles which I can use later on for spaghetti. Odelia, who is in charge of the restaurant at the diamond mines, brought me about 50 lbs of meat on Saturday which I put in the deep freeze. I have hamburger, roasts, liver, kidney, and even a leg of pork. I probably have the best stock of all the missions in Shinyanga diocese. Very few missions have electricity. A few have kerosene refrigerators which work very well. Fr. Charles Callahan, the chaplain of the mines, got me acquainted with Odelia and also her husband who is in charge of all the engineering at the mines. For about a week I didn't have water. Valerian sent a crew over to fix a broken pipe some place between here and the mines. Now the water supply is normal. I have started a small garden and so far have put in some beans and some carrots. This week I want to plant the squash seeds that our cousin, Marilyn Longen, gave me. With the water supply normal, I will be able to water the garden. My houseboy, Charles, is helping me with the planting and watering.

On Saturday I went to Shinyanga town which is 18 miles away and visited the market. There were quite a few fruits and vegetables available, much to my surprise. I got spinach, potatoes, tomatoes, bananas, papaya, and even some peanuts. So, as you can see, I am doing quite well and have plenty to eat.

I wrote to Dorothy asking if she could send me by airmail black-out curtains for the library. I would like to begin showing films in my library where I do most of my teaching. If she can get the material like I used at the Youth Center in Dar, it is light in weight and will still keep the light out. Maybe you could put in a couple of small containers of cinnamon and one of nutmeg. I have been making some cinnamon rolls and would like to make some apple pie, but have just a little cinnamon left which Fr. Bill left behind.

This is my third week of teaching. I had two classes this morning. Also, I am getting acquainted with the teachers on the staff. We have tea and coffee together in the staff room at 11 A.M. while the students are having their tea break. I was able to get some lux soap from Brother Cyril in Shinyanga which I sold to the teachers at cost. They were very happy about that since hand soap is almost impossible to get. Also, I got several cases of laundry soap, the bar type, called Sunlite, which John Lange has imported from Europe. This we sold to the students. Never realized how a bar of soap could make people so happy.

There are lots of things I would like to explain, but it's kind of hard to put it all in a letter. I am thinking one of these nights that I will make you a tape.... My greetings to all...

Love,

Fr. Marv

Footnote:

Why the broken water pipe? There was a large water pipe coming from the Diamond Mines to the Secondary School. However, unfortunately it was on the surface. The natives were always looking for water for their cattle. They frequently pierced the pipe and let the water flood out for their cattle. It was a never ending task to keep this pipe repaired.

Shinyanga Secondary School

August 21, 1982

Dear Mom,

This is Saturday morning and I am at Buhangija, the Diocesan center located about I mile out side of the town of Shinyanga. Saturday is a good time to come since I have no classes to teach and can do some shopping at the market. Today I changed the oil in my V.W. and also got help to fix a flat tire. Brother Cyril has all the equipment which makes this job much easier.

It has been a good week. I took over the English classes for Form I since they have no teacher. I teach 125 boys three times a week. There should be only 40 in each class but I do not have time to teach the same thing 3 times.

There are a couple of hundred broken chairs all stashed in the carpenter shop of the school which is right next store to me. There is such a shortage of chairs that the boys hide them so when they need them they suddenly appear. Some boys carry their chairs around with them from class to class. One boy was hiding 2 chairs in our center library. I caught him and forbade him to bring the school chairs to the Chaplain's Center library. All our chairs are in good condition and I don't want them confused. I hope to organize a group of boys interested in repairing the school chairs. I have a design substituting a wooden frame replacing the metal spokes. I have been trying to get wood and have stopped in the lumber company in town every Saturday, but so far nothing is available. Everything takes time.

I am making you a tape and will send it along with Fr. Tom Shea who will be going to the U.S. at the beginning of September. I have also taken a roll of pictures which I will send to Sr. Leonarda for developing and ask her to send you some prints.

Please tell Dorothy that I received her letter and will say the masses requested and send out a card....Greetings to all....
Love and Prayers,
Fr. Marv

Fr. John Lange, the VW kombi, and my dog Raha, on the day we arrived

Fr. Bill Tokus (the founding Father of the center) with Archbishop Mihayo who came for confirmations of the students. This was several years before my arrival.

Left: The center library where I did my teaching
Right: Our center Chapel - designed by Maryknoller, Brother Damien, (John Walsh)

The Chair Project

It was interesting to experience the cooperation I received in trying to solve the chair shortage in the school. There were 600 boys in the school but only 400 chairs. If you look at the picture in the lower right, you will see many broken chair parts, especially the metal legs. Using the plastic tops, I made a number of wooden legs as you can see in the upper picture. But the going was too slow. And so we decided to make stools or little benches, which were simple and relatively easy to make. Dave, (lower left picture) the volunteer from England, was one of the best workers. Larry Radiche, a Maryknoll seminarian, on his overseas training, also helped. He is in the first picture. Some students and a couple of teachers also pitched in.

Fr. Charles Callahan - Chaplain at the mines

Odelia and her husband, the head engineer at the mines

Students in our library

Left: The headmaster, Mr. Masaki and I - He was congratulating me for the work I had done for the school.
Right: Gedi - one of the school employees. He brought my mail every day.

Shinyanga Secondary School

Sept. 15, 1982
Our Lady of Sorrows

Dear Mom,

Fr. Tom shea took the tape I made for you as well as the film to be developed by Sister Leonarda, to the States with him. I figure you should get the tape about this time, Sept. 15th or so. Sr. Leonarda will send you copies of the pictures. I just heard from her. She sent me copies of pictures that I had taken in N.Y. That's a handy service.

This past week we were without electricity for 5 days. The Mwadui mine's people ran out of lubricating oil for their big diesel generators. I loaded my little deep freeze in the V.W. Van and brought it over to Fr. Charles, the chaplain at the mine. He is on the special circuit with other essentials like the hospital and post office. I have a regular fridge besides with an adequate freezing compartment and so if the electricity comes on I can use it for everyday things. Fr. Charles is only about 15 minutes away. I can go through the back gate since I am now well-known over there. The kids can't study after dark which is about 7 P.M. while the electricity is turned off. That's part of life over here. Sometimes there is no water and sometimes no electricity. Life goes on and there seem to be few complaints.

I am now meeting 2 afternoons a week with about 20 boys in the carpenter shop. We have about a dozen chairs finished. The school needs a couple of hundred, but slowly slowly we are improving the situation.

Fr. Jim Travis arrived yesterday afternoon and is with me now. He is originally from the Archdiocese of St. Paul. I knew him when he was stationed at White Bear. He got permission from Archbishop Byrne to join Maryknoll. Jim is stationed at Mwamapalala parish about 75 miles from here. He is on a few days vacation and is traveling around by motor bike.

I am happy to hear you have your loom working again. I have your rugs all over the house and they are sure nice to have......My greetings to all. Deb will be having a birthday soon. Just a year ago when we celebrated her birthday with a fish dinner. Seems like a lot has happened since then.....I am happy to hear that Ethel Jeroui is making the blackout curtains for our library. By now perhaps they are already on the way.

Love, Fr. Marv

Shinyanga Secondary School

Oct. 15, 1982

Dear Mom,

Your letters of Sept. 27 and 29 arrived yesterday. I am happy you received the audio-tape which gives you a good idea of what life is like here. The last couple of weeks there has been very little trouble with the electricity. It is off for a few hours now and then, but that is no big problem. Fr. Charles at Mwadui Mines has gone on vacation and so I have brought my little deep freeze back home and all is well.

There has been no school the last two days. Everyone is preparing for the Form IV graduation which takes place tomorrow. They have a different system here. Although the term is not finished until early December, graduation takes place now. After graduation the students do not leave the school, but have no more formal classes. The form IV students spend their time from now until the end of the term preparing for final examinations which begin after the middle of November. So really graduation doesn't mean all that much. It just means that they have put in their 4 years. But how they do in their examinations determine if they will be chosen for the next step of education which is form V or equivalent to our first year of college.

Last Tuesday there was a big celebration in Shinyanga at the Bishop's place to honor my 25th anniversary and also to say goodbye to Fr. Richard Hochwalt who is leaving Tanzania after 25 years for a new assignment in the treasury department at Maryknoll, N.Y. I was really surprised. After all the celebrations at home, I didn't expect another out here. It was all organized by the African priests and sisters, and just about all the African priests and sisters in the diocese showed up, which would number about 40. They also had a big choir of about 80 youth and a number of lay people. After a concelebrated mass with Bishop Castor Sekwa, there was a display of dancing and singing by the African youth and quite a few speeches which the Africans love. The African sisters also prepared a big dinner which was served cafeteria style. I was happy to celebrate the occasion with Fr. Hochwalt. He is a few years older than I am, but we came out on the same ship in 1957.

As I mentioned in my last letter to Dorothy, the curtains arrived and I had to pay no duty. Dorothy said you paid for the postage. Thanks very much, Mom. The curtains are really nice. I am working on putting up the rods now. I have the wood supports almost finished and will have them up soon.

I have to reserve some space to wish you a HAPPY BIRTHDAY. I will be saying mass for you on your day. I would call if it would be more convenient to do so, but communication between here and the international system in Dar is very poor. We can contact Dar, but it often takes hours for the call to go through. Anyhow, I wish you the very best on your day and I thank God he has given you good health. May your day be full of surprises. Much love always,

Fr. Marv

Shinyanga Secondary School

Oct. 24, 1982

Dear Mom,

This is Sunday afternoon. It is recreation time for the boys here at the center. Some are playing cards, others listening to music, reading magazines, etc. I am going to show them a film in our library after a while. I finished putting up the curtains yesterday and showed the first film this morning to the group of boys studying for Baptism. The curtains look very attractive and serve very well in keeping out the light. I am happy that Ethel made them wider than I specified. It's a perfect fit.

Yesterday we had a torrential rainfall, more like a cloud burst. I put out a couple of plastic buckets to catch water to use for my car battery. The buckets had more than 4 inches of water in them which gives a pretty good idea of how much rain we got in just 2 hours. In a few days we should see the country- side turning green. I put in a half dozen papaya seedlings and one mango tree a few days ago. I planted the seeds about 2 months ago and they are now about 4 inches high. I plan to put in about a dozen more fruit trees before the month is over. Papaya trees bear fruit after about 9 months which is quite amazing. The rain is very welcome and earlier than usual. There are hundreds of cows going by here every day in search for the bits of grass that remain. They are also being led to Songwa dam about 3 miles from here where there is still plenty of water. Some of the cows have been brought from over 50 miles away where the grass is completely gone and the water supply finished.

In your letter you mentioned that Sr. Leonarda sent you the pictures which I took around here. She sent me prints too which arrived a few days ago. I put them up on the bulletin board today. In one picture you see boys digging holes. They are members of the vocation club, boys interested in the priesthood. They dug those holes two months ago in preparation for putting in the seedlings which I mentioned above. From the pictures you can see all the trees and shrubbery around the church and my house.

The electricity has been steady for 2 weeks. Thanks be to God for little favors. That's about all the news that I can think of. I want to write a few lines to Sr. Leonarda too, to thank her for sending the pictures.

I hope you had a nice birthday...
Much love,
Fr. Marv

Footnote:

None of the trees that we planted reached maturity. The goats and the cows got them since there is no fencing anywhere except around the diamond mines. One papaya tree almost made it. It got to be about 4 feet high. One day I was in the sacristy looking out the window and I saw a cow chomp off the whole top of the tree. The shepherd boy didn't seem to be watching.

Shinyanga Secondary School

Nov. 4, 1982

Dear Mom,

I was very surprised to hear about Floyds open heart surgery since I don't remember him complaining about chest pains. Perhaps by now he is already out of the hospital and doing fine. I have been remembering him at mass every day.

We have been having a great deal of rain. In fact, just about every day we get some kind of a shower. The whole countryside is green - just like springtime. The flowers are out; the trees are shooting out leaves, and the grass is green. In all my years out here, this is the earliest I can remember this much rain in the Shinyanga area this early. The big herds of cattle around here are snapping up the green grass as soon as it hits the surface. I can hear a few cows mooing right now with their cow bells clanging as they mosey along.

The boys in the vocation club will be coming at 4 P.M. to help me plant some more papaya trees. If I can get in about a dozen more, there should be plenty of Papaya around here about a year from now. On your birthday I celebrated by having the first squash from the seeds I got from our cousin Marilyn. I baked it in the oven and it really was excellent.

After it is cooked, it shreds up something like spaghetti. I am spreading the seeds around to others so perhaps we can introduce something new to Africa.

I am happy to hear that John and Margaret are still together. It's a big sacrifice that you and Dorothy have to make, but if somehow they can stick together, it is probably worth it. You mentioned that your house is full of their furniture. Maybe you could have some of the stuff put in your garage to make more room.

School is going along really well. I now show movies regularly as part of the teaching program, thanks to the new curtains which work perfectly in blocking out the light.....It is time to fight down the dough and put it into loaves. I am going to make some cinnamon bread too with the supply of cinnamon that came with the curtains.... Greetings and best wishes to all.

Love,

Fr. Marv

Footnote:

Floyd Johnson was my twin sister's husband. He died of Parkinson's in the year 2000.

Margaret was the adopted daughter of my older sister, Dorothy. From day one of their marriage, she and John never got along. As I see it now, John had some psychological and emotional problems which made it impossible for him to love Margaret in a self-sacrificing way.

About 20 years down the line, Margaret got an annulment and eventually found a good man to marry. I was happy about that especially to know how much Margaret suffered in her previous marriage.

Shinyanga Secondary School

Nov. 21, 1982
Feast of Christ the King

Dear Mom,

I think it is about 2 weeks since I have written to you. I wrote to Marlys last week and so, no doubt, she has told you about my letter.

This is kind of an extra busy time since there are only 2 weeks left of school. We had a beautiful celebration today for the feast of Christ the King. The choir from Mwadui Diamond Mines came for mass. Thus we had two choirs. They alternated with ours, each taking a different part of the mass. Fr. Dave Schwinghammer, Maryknoller who is our regional coordinator, was here for the weekend. He was the main celebrant and I gave the homily.

Today, also, I began interviewing and questioning the boys who are in the catechumenate (convert class). There are about 25 of them. Those who pass and I expect they all will, will receive a rosary at a little ceremony which will take place at next Sunday's mass. This means that they are one step closer to Baptism, but still have a ways to go.

Dorothy asked if I had received the box which I sent while home last June. I finally received notice yesterday that the package is waiting at the Mwadui Mines post office. I plan to go over tomorrow to pick it up. That took a long time - 5 months. I am happy it has arrived since it contains a large quantity of yeast. I still have a couple of packets left, but am close to the end. I have plenty of flour now so will be able to continue to make bread which is totally unavailable, even at the mines these days.

The rains have let up a little. It hasn't rained now for 4 days., but the county side is beautiful and green. I planted some more things - sweet potatoes and sweet corn. I got the seeds for the sweet corn from Brother John Wohead who returned recently from the U.S.

I have another little dog to take care of now. An English gal, Ann, who teaches here, went back to England for 2 months and asked me to take care of her puppy which is 4 months old and extremely active. It is kind of cute but is at the destructive stage when it wants to chew on everything.
Till next week.... Lots of love....
Fr. Marv

Shinyanga Secondary School
December 15, 1982

Dear Mom,

Here it is the middle of December and I'm just starting my Christmas letters. The school year is over now (my first as chaplain here) and the boys have gone home for vacation - all except for 40 of the Form I's who will be here for 3 weeks to take care of the school and the grounds. When they leave, another group will come for the remainder of the vacation period.

Besides teaching all the religion classes this past term, I also taught form I English since they had no teacher and so much of their future education depends on their knowledge of English. I just finished correcting 110 final examinations and was rather pleased. All the blind students were in the upper 10%. I had given their exam orally.

The last six weeks has been the rainiest time for this period since the great rains of 1961-62. It usually isn't this green until March or April. It rains almost every day in the late afternoon or early evening. Sometimes it rains half the night. This is very un-Tanzania like. The crops are doing splendidly. The corn is already over a foot high in places. I think the Lord is smiling on us and having mercy on these long suffering people. They haven't had a good crop in years.

I also have my garden planted - corn, potatoes, peanuts, squash and tomatoes. With supplies so difficult to get, these things will be a real asset in the future. With the help of the boys I put in some papaya trees. I had started the seeds several months ago, and now they are a foot high. Papaya trees are quite remarkable. They usually start bearing fruit in about 9 months time . The fruit is excellent for breakfast.

So far I haven't minded living alone even though it is quite isolated here from the rest of the world. We have no telephone and letters take about 3 weeks. Maybe in one way it is a blessing. We have our own problems, but the many worries of the Western world don't seem to affect us much. I am very grateful for my small chapel and the presence of our Lord in the Blessed Sacrament. I spend a lot of time with him, which is a great consolation.

I guess that is what the meaning of Christmas is all about - the presence of our Lord in our midst. But we have to be quiet to hear him. He doesn't talk with a loud voice, but he is really there and whispers into our hearts when we are ready and open to receive him. And so this Christmas I wish you the joy of his presence, the greatest of all joys that man can experience. You are included in my masses and prayers this Christmas season and every day in the New Year.

Peace, love and prayers,

Fr. Marv

Footnote:

The above was my Christmas letter to my family and friends. A word about the blind students: The government was trying an experiment. Instead of sending them to a school just for the blind, they were mixed in with the ordinary students. They had a couple of special classes taught in braille, but other than that, mixed right in. These students did quite well. They knew how to get around the campus without canes. Of the 600 students, about 20 were blind. As time went on, I was able to do a lot for them as you will see in future letters.

Shinyanga Secondary School

Dec. 29, 1982

Dear Mom,

Thank you for your Christmas letter which arrived on Dec. 24th, also for the picture of Jack's family which is quite charming. I hope your Christmas was a joyful one filled with many blessings. Mine was rather quiet since the form I boys who were left behind to take care of the school, left on Dec. 24th, and some on early Christmas morning before mass. Only the workers with their families and a couple of teachers were here for mass. After mass I showed the beautiful film on the Life of Christ, the section on the birth of the Savior which added a great deal to the celebration.

The other half of the form I boys have returned now to take care of the property until school starts on January 15th. A group of them were just at my door wanting the results of their English exam. I told them they should all come together and I will give them back and go over the exam with them at the same time so they can correct their mistakes.

A couple of days ago, the head master, Mr. Masaki, dropped in for a visit. I was surprised to see him since it was the first time he has come to my house. He was very appreciative for the work I did for the school this past term, especially with my English class and helping the boys to repair some of the chairs. This coming term he said he has an

English teacher for Form I and Form II which will give me more time for my religion classes.

The rains have slowed down. There has just been one good rain in the last 10 days, but the crops are doing well. I hope we get a few good rains in January to keep things growing. I am happy to have a little time to take it easy. There are many things around here that need repair. Yesterday I fixed some of the locks and doors which were not functioning properly. In one of the door locks I found that spiders and bugs had laid their eggs and left so much dirt inside that it couldn't possibly work. I also want to make a book rack for the chapel. We have books to use for prayer and meditation. Everything is so messy when just thrown on a table.

Please tell Dorothy that I received her letter on Christmas eve. I will say the mass for Betty Lou Uram and send out a card. Hi to Debbie. The best to you and all in the New Year...

Much love,

Fr. Marv

Footnote:

Betty Lou Uram was a grade school classmate. She died suddenly.

The above pictures were taken of our neighbors near the secondary school. The Africans like to have fun when they are working. In the middle picture, the people lined up in a row, are all swinging their hoes to the beat of the drum. I could see they were having a very good time. The top picture is a little girl who is standing in a field of millet. Millet is resistant to drought and can withstand 3 or 4 weeks without rain. It is planted as a safeguard just in case the rains are not sufficient for the corn crop. Millet can be ground into flour just as corn is. However, it is not as well liked as corn.

Shinyanga Secondary School

January 10, 1983

Dear Mom,

Thanks for your letter of Dec. 6th which arrived about a week ago. Shortly after the middle of December, the rains stopped. It was completely dry for about 2 weeks. Under the hot sun, the corn which was over a foot high, began to shrivel up. But on Jan. 2nd the rains came back again. It rained on Jan. 2nd, 3rd, and 6th, all good rains. So now the crops are looking beautiful again. During this vacation time, I have really enjoyed working in my garden, which is about half the size of your lot. I have been getting tomatoes and squash for a long time now and the sweet corn is just beginning to tassel out. I put in some yellow wax beans about a week ago and I noticed this morning that they are just beginning to peep through the surface.

During the vacation period I wanted to visit Fr. Dan Ohmann at Ndoleleji mission which is about 45 miles from here, but there has been a shortage of gasoline. The railway tankers usually come to Shinyanga town to keep this area supplied, but one of the railway bridges went out because of the heavy rains. To my knowledge it has not yet been repaired. I don't know how serious the damage is.

This vacation period has been a restful time for me. There are about 40 of the form I boys who come to the center every afternoon for recreation. They haven't been any problem for me. They use the center for card playing and reading. I put them to work for an hour a week to keep the center looking nice. They clean the church and cut the grass around the center with grass slashers. I noticed over around the school it looks like a forest since now the grass is about 2 feet high. All the boys will be coming back at the end of this week. The first couple of days, no doubt, will be spent in getting the grounds shaped up.

A lot of my Christmas mail is coming in now. I finally got my letters mailed on Christmas day. By now most people will have heard from me. Next week I will be on retreat which I will make at Wila Mission which is 20 miles from there. I think there will be about 10 Maryknollers making their retreat there. Classes don't start in earnest until the following week anyway, and so it will be a good way to start out the new school year.

I hope this finds you feeling well and the weather not so cold. Give my hello to Dorothy, Marlys and all....
Much love,
Fr. Marv

Students enjoying our library

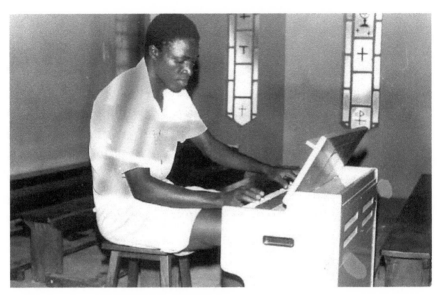

Our small pump organ in the chapel

A couple of the students and I in the corn field

This is how meals are prepared for the students - The cooking pot is filled with corn flour and water which is boiled over a charcoal stove until stiff. The finished product is called "ugali".

An upper class student with a 2 story classroom block in the background

Shinyanga Secondary School

Feb. 19, 1983

Dear Mom,

Many thanks for your letters of Jan. 26 and Feb. 2. I think I slipped up on my letter to you last week. I get so busy at times that time slips away. It is great to hear that Jack can help you with the repairs. Everything mechanical wears out. With a few good Germans around, things can be kept humming.

We received very good rain this morning beginning about 6 AM lasting until 10 AM. I am sure there was at least an inch. I would say we received about half this much a week ago. Things dry up so fast in the very hot sun that one rain a week is just enough to keep the crops from burning off. The crops still look pretty good. They would be better if it hadn't been for a 3 week spell in late January and early February when there was no rain. My peanuts, corn and tomatoes have done well. I am eating corn now and have had tomatoes for a long time. The peanuts will be ready in about 3 more weeks.

I took some pictures and sent them to Sr. Leonarda for developing. I am sure she will send you some. She was interested in how they can feed 600 boys here on charcoal burners.

I now have a bicycle. I ordered one 2 years ago. Fr. John Lange sent it up from Dar. It is not a 10 speed, but *rides just as easily. John had ordered a number from England, but some of the boxes had been broken into. Anyhow it is nice to have. I take it out for a half hour several times a week. My dog, Raha, trails along side. These back trails are good for biking.*

Lent has begun. I have a special Lenten mass for the students on Wednesday and Stations of the Cross on Friday. We are now using the rite for confessions which have more scripture. I see the pope in trying to get Catholics to go back using private confession again with the inauguration of the Holy Year beginning March 25th. I have been pushing private confession and have had pretty good results.

Next week we have a priests' Senate Meeting in Shinyanga for all the priests of the diocese. Since I am the secretary, I have quite a bit of extra work to do. I am glad we only meet twice a year.

Here's wishing you a happy Lent, Mom. I hope your weather is getting nicer now. From what I hear your winter was not so bad. Sometimes when that happens you get all the bad weather in the spring.

Much love,
Fr. Marv
P.S. *I received a nice letter from Sr. Ellen Joseph*

Footnote:

Some of the priests had abandoned private confession and were offering general absolution. This was true of my predecessor at Shinyanga Secondary School. It took quite a while to get the students used to going back to private confession.

Sr. Ellen Joseph was my 8th grade teacher at St. Helena's grade school in Minneapolis. She was a wonderful nun. In 8th grade she told me she thought I had a vocation to the priesthood although I didn't enter the seminar till 3rd year college.

Shinyanga Secondary School

March 5, 1983

Dear Mom,

I missed writing last week because of a few extra jobs I had to do. Bishop Castor asked me to help him write his pastoral letter initiating the Holy Year the Holy Father is calling for, beginning on March 25th. I had to do quite a bit of study and research, but the work is done now. I think it will be a big help to the diocese in the year ahead.

I am writing this letter from Buhangija parish which is about a mile outside of Shinyanga town and about 18 miles from my school. It is not only a parish but sort of a center house for the diocese. The bishop also lives here. I stayed here overnight just to get a little change.

Last weekend Fr. Dan Ohmann stayed with me. He came in from his parish, Ndoleleji. He has not been feeling well, is very tired and run down. He is due for home leave this June anyways and so decided to go home a couple of months early. By now he has probably already left Dar es Salaam for the U.S.

The weather has been quite dry. We have had a little rain about once a week for the past month, but really not enough. People are already harvesting the crop that was put in early November and have done pretty well in spite of the dry spell this past month. The long rains usually begin about March 15th. We will see if they come on time this year. If they do, many people will plant a second time.

There seems to be a lot of sickness around. Brother Cyril is in bed right now suffering from malaria. I have been lucky. I try to get sufficient rest which is the most important preventive there is, and I also take my malaria pills regularly.

Pope John Paul is on his visit to Central America these days. We get the news via radio BBC (British Broadcasting Company). Hope this finds all well. Happy Springtime, and thanks for the Valentine's greetings.
Much love,
Fr. Marv

Sunday, April 10, 1983
Dear Mom,
I want to thank you for your letters of March 7 and 20. It has been a couple of weeks since I have written. I just haven't had time to sit down and compose a letter. I had so

many things to do in preparation for Holy Week plus quite a few other tasks to do. In my spare time I did a 10 page position paper to represent the Maryknollers in the Shinyanga area. This is for the regional meeting in June to be held at Musoma. I got that finished before the beginning of Holy Week. The past few days I have been preparing a talk to be given for a recollection day this coming Tuesday to the Shinyanga deanery which includes the African and Maryknoll Fathers together. I have that ready too now, so I can sit down to write a few letters.

There hasn't been any school for a week and a half. The boys who live nearby could go home for Easter. There were about 60 who were here for the Holy Week services, which came off very well. The last couple of days have been sport days with various teams from neighboring areas coming here for soccer, volleyball, basketball and track. Fr. Jim Travis brought a number of T shirts and track shorts which he received from the U.S. They were left over from the 1979 Olympic Games. I am selling them very cheaply. There are not enough for everybody, but at least we can outfit the various teams representing the school. Classes begin tomorrow. I have most of the extra jobs done and so I hope I can settle down to a normal schedule for the 2nd half of the term.

Fr. Jim Travis is going home in about 2 week's time. His address is 2417 E. 12th Ave; North St. Paul 55109. Phone 777 1883. Fr. Jim and I and two others are going in together in sending over a container through Brother Regis in New

Holstein, Wisconsin. I don't think I will have to use any of the money in my Mpls. Account. I am writing to New York asking them to send him money from my mission account. I have asked Jim to stop in to see you and pick up the electric drill which I left behind which you will find in my box upstairs. I think there are some attachments for it with the drill that can go with it. Also, if you have any of those light homemade blankets which you don't need, give those to Fr. Jim, too.. The blankets on my 3 beds here are really shot. I need either 3 light blankets or quilts. Two of the beds are 3 ft. wide and one is 3 1/2 ft. wide. Fr. Jim has agreed to do the shopping. I think Fr. Nygard from Egan will get someone to help him. It will be quite a job since there are 4 of us with lists.

The pictures and the yeast have not yet arrived. No doubt they are being held up because if there is anything besides pictures, it has to go through customs. But there's no rush. We are all here and not going any place.

The weather has been very dry. The long rains failed to come. I hope we get at least 2 weeks of rain before the real dry season comes...

Love,
Fr. Marv

Footnote:

The 10 page position paper I wrote had to do with preparation for the forthcoming chapter in 1984. There was a great concern for the dwindling numbers in Maryknoll and the lack of vocations to the priesthood. The lay missionary movement was thought by many to be the future of our Maryknoll Society. Also Liberation Theology was being advocated by most of our men in South American. My paper, which I did with the consultation with Fr. Richard Hochwalt (who had a doctorate in Canon Law), was an attempt to show that Rome would never agree for lay missionaries to become members of our Society. I also tried to show that Liberation Theology was politicizing the gospel and deemphasizing the spiritual goal of the Church which is salvation. My paper was not accepted, although eventually it was sent out to all members of Maryknoll. One group in Bolivia even sent it to Cardinal Tomko in Rome (head of the Congregation for the Propagation of the Faith and therefore our boss) stating that this paper was an excellent portrayal of what was wrong with Maryknoll. As it turned out, the chapter approved the entrance of lay people into our society. When the constitutional change to allow this was presented to Rome, it was turned down.

Shinyanga Secondary School

April 21, 1983

Dear Mom and Dorothy,

I want to send this to both of you since I am sure you both had a hand in preparing the package which I received two days ago. The package took a couple of weeks longer than your letters because it had to go through customs, but it arrived in perfect condition. One of the boys has kind of a business going and sells pictures to the other boys who want their picture taken. He took all the color pictures. The black and whites are mine. Thanks much for sending the yeast and the seeds. That's a good way to send them especially because they are so light. I am not going to plant the seeds right away because there is no rain. The long rains which usually come in March and April did not come this year. This is the driest April that I have ever experienced in Tanzania.

Last week I started out on a trip to Tabora which is 125 miles south of Shinyanga. I wanted to visit the Catholic bookshop there to buy bibles and other books for the students. But I just got about 50 miles from here when the front shock absorber on my van went out. The road was very corrugated and the shock finally gave out. After 5 years on these roads, one was sure to go. I came back home very slowly and made it o.k. I have some spares here but I see the bushing which fits on to the bolt on the frame is a little bit too small. I am having the bushing reamed out at the workshop at Mwadui Mines which I hope to pick up today. It should work o.k.

Last Saturday we had graduation here for the form 6 boys. Although they don't take their exams until the middle of May, the graduation ceremony is always held early. I suppose this is done so it won't interfere with the exam preparations. The boys from the other forms put on skits and songs. The blind boys' singing group was the best. I hope to record some of their songs a little later. These boys never cease to amaze me - how they do so well in spite of their handicap.

I am going to Mwadui now to mail this...Bye for now...
Much love and payers,
Fr. Marv

Shinyanga Secondary School

May 3, 1983

Dear Mom,

I hear you had a big snow storm on April 14th. That's amazing. The rainy season never materialized here. This past month we had about 1 rain a week, but that is nothing compared to the normal amount for April. The dry season sets in about now with cooler weather and high winds. It is cooler already in the morning. We may get one or two more rains, but after May 15th, there is usually nothing until next fall.

There has been a big drive by the government to crack down on smugglers. Many of the Arab shops in the nearby town of Maganzo were searched. One of the Arabs was found with over two pounds of diamonds. I don't know how much two pounds is worth, but it is certainly in the hundreds of thousands of dollars. Some of the Africans were picked up too. Some had stashed away huge quantities of sugar, salt, and cooking oil, and of course making huge profits on the black market. Whenever there is a big shortage of goods, there will be such problems.

I have most of my extra jobs for the diocese done now, which will give me a little more time for leisure. I really like to do carpentry work for recreation, but since January I haven't had any time. Yesterday I made an outdoor flower box to get back into the swing of things. I also want to help the boys make more chairs. There really isn't much time left of the school year, or I should say, for the first half. School closes for over a month beginning on June 4th. We have our meeting in Musoma for all Maryknollers from June 7 to 11th. After that I plan to fly to Dar for a couple of weeks vacation.

Greetings and best wishes to all.....
Much love,
Fr. Marv

Footnote:

Stealing diamonds was not such an easy task. There were two rows of fences encircling the whole diamond mine town. At night vicious German shepherd dogs were on patrol with their masters between the fences. That so many diamonds could be stolen seems to indicate that it must have been an inside job. Several times men came to my house in an effort to sell me some diamonds. I refused to have anything to do with them.

The failure of the rains in 1983 was a very bad omen for the future. 1984 turned out to be a year of disaster. Famine was just around the corner. The government was encouraging the people to plant millet which is much more resistant to drought than corn. However, the people were slow to respond which would bring about a much greater crisis than would have been otherwise.

Shinyanga Secondary School

July 12, 1983

Dear Mom,

Today is a national holiday in honor of the end of the Moslem month-long fast called Ramadan. All is quiet. Only about a hundred of the 600 students have returned. There is a serious gasoline and diesel shortage in the country. Very few buses are running and the train which comes from Dar to Shinyanga is only running 3 times a week instead of the usual 7. Some of the boys who live fairly close have walked back to school. One boy yesterday told me that he walked from his parent's place which is 20 miles away. Tanzania just doesn't have enough foreign exchange to buy the crude oil they need to run the country. Some fuel supplies will be coming in, but it seems there will be a shortage for a long time to come. I was able to buy a few gallons of gas at the Mwadui Diamond Mines pump which enables me to get to Shinyanga and back and to drive over to the mines.

I have my living room fixed up real cozy now. I painted one wall a smoke blue color which I mixed myself with tube coloring and also reupholstered one of the worn sofas with a beautiful rust brown material which I had been saving. I think you remember when Dorothy and I packed that upholstery material some years ago for our house in Dar es Salaam. I still have some rich looking pieces left.

I have my class schedule which has much better hours than last term. Dave Ecklund, the English volunteer who teaches chemistry, is in charge of making out the class schedules. He did a good job in giving me some good periods. Last term I had some periods at 1 P.M. in the afternoon which is the last period of the day when everyone is sleepy. We will probably begin teaching toward the end of the week as more students return.

The mail seems slower than ever because of the transportation problem. The last letter I have of yours is June 4, although I am sure there are others on the way. There is lots of celebrating at St. Helena's this year with both Fr. Duffy and Fr. Villano celebrating their 25th anniversaries. Leave it to Duffy to think of something different. I hear he is having his reception in the parking lot. He always was an outdoors' man. Fr. John Lange will be around Minneapolis during the month of August. No doubt he will stop in to see you. He will be taking a renewal course in California later on in the fall.

Will say bye for now.... Greetings to all...
Love and prayers,
Fr. Marv

Footnote:
Foreign exchange refers to money that can be used on the international market. Dollars, Deutsch Marks, English pounds and Japanese yen, are all usable. Tanzania

Shillings are not. Tanzania needs to sell exports to get Foreign Exchange. Grants from other countries is another way of getting Foreign Exchange.

Fr. Duffy was my classmate at St. Thomas College. Fr. Villano was the pastor at our home parish of St. Helena's.

Shinyanga Secondary School

August 19, 1983

Dear Mom,

I have your letters of July 18, July 28, and August 7. The packet of photos arrived some time ago and I have given them out to the people concerned which made them very happy.

I was over at the diamond mines this morning arranging to have some wood planed so we can make more stools for the classrooms. The engineer in charge of the shop there is very helpful, and he is not charging. They have all kinds of equipment there and can do just about anything. They even cut their own logs, make doors, windows and beautiful furniture. When you see some of these things you almost forget that you are out in the bush in Tanzania which shows that it can be done. Most of the engineers there have been trained outside the country in places like England, the U.S. or Canada.

I expect the container that Fr. Jim Travis sent through Brother Regis sometime in September. The Diamond mines' people have agreed to help me with the transport of the container. The container will be arriving in Dar es Salaam. It will be put on a flat car and come by rail all the way to the Diamond mines. They have a huge mobile crane which will lift it off the freight car, and put it on a wagon. Then a tractor will pull it over here. The crane will come too and lift it off the wagon and set it upon a foundation which I have already built with the help of a few students. The container once emptied will make a wonderful store room.

A supply of sugar came in both to the school and to the diamond mines a few days ago. The school was out of sugar and out of corn flour. The boys usually have what they call "uji" for breakfast, which is corn flour mixed with sugar, cooked into a sort of porridge which looks like cream of wheat. When they had no flour or sugar, they were eating beans. Since the beans take so long to cook, the cooks had to get up in the middle of the night to prepare them. Using charcoal fires, it is no easy task. Life struggles on here. I am fortunate that I have my own supplies and don't have to spend so much time trying to buy something.

Your summer is just about over. Our season here is still cool enough to be comfortable. There is no rain of course this time of year, but our water supply from the mines is ample. A while back the cow herders were punching holes in the 6" pipe which comes from the mines, in order to get water for their cattle, but the holes in the pipe have been repaired and the people warned. There has been no problem the past month.

Best wishes to all....
Love and prayers,
Fr. Marv

Shinyanga Secondary School

September 25, 1983

Dear Mom,

Many thanks for your letter of Aug. 17. There is probably another letter at the P.O. now which will probably come in a day or two, explaining the sisters' visit. .

This past week has been the mid-term break, but I was ever so busy. On Sept. 14th our container arrived here at the school. It was just getting dark and I was returning from the priests' senate meeting in Shinyanga. As I was coming down the road leading to my place, I see all this machinery coming towards me with a big red container in the middle of it all. It arrived unexpectedly. I had called Dar a week before. They thought it was still on the high seas. Evidently when Ed Philips, our procurator went home on leave in July, he had left instructions with our worker, Edward, who took care of the whole thing. Anyhow, I was glad to see it. Mwadui mines agreed to bring it here from Songwa rail station, which is about 5 miles away. They have all the equipment including a big flatbed trailer and a mobile crane. The container weighed 19 tons and was brought here fully loaded and lifted on to the ground right at my place. It was too dark the night they came to set it on the foundation which we had prepared, but they came back two days later after we had emptied it, and set it up. They also brought another empty one which Brother Cyril had given to me, and set that up too. Now I have plenty of storage space and will use one of the containers as a small classroom after it is modified somewhat. I plan to put in a door and a couple of windows. I took pictures of the whole operation with all the machinery. Later on I will send the film to Sr. Leonarda who no doubt will send the pictures on to you.

Also, during the mid-term break, a couple of teachers and students helped me build 3 dozen stools. We finished them yesterday, applying a coat of varnish. I also used the drill you sent and tools and screws which were in the container.... I want to thank you for the nice blankets, nice and light, just right for out here.

Yesterday Fr. Herb Gappa sent his 7 ton truck to pick up contents of the container designated for Musoma and other missions. I had been using my library as a sorting out place so I am happy to get rid of everything. The boys came this afternoon to rearrange and clean up the library so we are ready for business again.

I am invited to Mwadui mines this evening. The women of the parish are having a celebration and since I help Fr. Charles, the chaplain, now and then, I have many friends there and am well known.

We should be getting our first rain one of these days. The humidity is building up. We have clouds and lots of wind, but no rain... Greetings to all.

Much love,

Fr. Marv

When the Mwadui Mines people brought over the container, it caused quite a bit of commotion among the students. Most of them had never seen anything like this before. I knew the general manager of the mines, Silvanus. He was most helpful and never charged me for any of their services. I had met him years earlier in 1958. When I received my first assignment to Sayusayu mission, Silvanus was a student in secondary school. He lived near Sayusayu and when he was on vacation, helped me write my sermons in the native language, Kisukuma.

The top picture shows the arrival of the container, on top of a wagon which was being pulled by a tractor. The bottom picture is the huge crane which lifted off the 19 ton container as if it was a toy.

It is interesting to see the progression of the container project. At the top left the containers are in place. The English volunteer, Dave Ecklund and Maryknoll seminarian, Larry Radiche, are standing in front; In the top picture on the right the work has begun to make the containers into little buildings; the middle picture on the left is myself with an African lad in the rear of the containers. A piece of the light aluminum sheeting for the roof is behind us. The middle picture on the right is Mike Dodd, the English volunteer who helped me put on the roof. The bottom two pictures show the work completed before and after the containers were painted. You can see the windows in the container to the left. I put electricity and lights in the containers. The one on the left was made into a club house for the blind students.

The containers became very solid little houses 20 ft long by 8 ft wide. I turned one of them into a club house for our 20 blind students. It was their place to do with what they wanted. Many came every day when school was out to do homework or to play games or practice their music. The bottom picture is of two blind boys doing their home work using braille. Note the paneled walls and the curtains. It was quite a deluxe place. The upper picture is composed of the blind boys' singing group. I got guitars for them. They were amazingly talented. It was quite remarkable how they could do so well being stone blind.

Shinyanga Secondary School

Oct. 22, 1983

Dear Mom,

Your letter of Sept. 28th arrived on Oct. 11. The mail service has been a little faster since the Mwadui Diamond Mines' plane began flying about a month ago. It was laid up for almost 2 years for lack of spare parts, but now it flies back and forth to Dar es Salaam twice a week.

I hope by now that Toni has recovered from her operation. Sr. j:anice Welle wrote that she also has had a hysterectomy. It seems to be a problem for many of that age group.

My place has caught on here as a place to come to relax. Quite a few Maryknollers have been coming to spend a day or two. Since I am the chief cook and bottle washer, it keeps me pretty busy. But I enjoy the company and since I am still stocked, the cooking is not that difficult. I was able to get a 6 week supply of meat from the Mwadui Mines butchery last week. I have an electric meat grinder which came in the container shipment and so it is easy to make my own hamburger.

Yesterday I had a penitential service in keeping with the spirit of the Holy Year. Fr. Charles Callahan from the mines and Fr. Jim Lenihan from the neighboring mission of Wila, came to help me with the confessions. About 60 boys came which I thought was very good. The Holy Father is trying to reestablish this sacrament among Catholics throughout the world which is a very good idea.

I have another film to send to Sr. Leonarda and so will write her a few lines too. Greetings to all.
Much love,
Fr. Marv

Saturday, December 31, 1983
Dear Mom,
This is the very last day of the year 1983. I want to get a few lines off to you to close out the old year in good fashion. I got behind in all my letter writing for Christmas because of the projects we were working on here the last 4 weeks. The roof on the container house is finished now. It really looks great and the space below will be useful for so many things in the New Year. Michael Dowd, the English

volunteer, supervised the repairs on 400 desks. And the other English volunteer, David, supervised the construction of 35 chairs following the design I had made. What we did has been very important for the school and the New Year should be so much better organized as regards each student having what he needs to study.

I have taken quite a few pictures of the work which you will see eventually when Sr. Leonarda gets the film.

We have had some wonderful rains the 2 weeks before Christmas ending a 9 month drought. The people who live nearby are out in the fields cultivating like mad. There is plenty of water right now and we hope that the rains continue.

I will get busy writing some New Year's letters. So many people who did not hear from me will still get a letter. I received new letters from Dorothy, Marlys and the sisters. Thank you very much for your Christmas card which arrived just before Christmas. I had a very nice Christmas.

Much love and many prayers in the New Year,
Fr. Marv

Shinyanga Secondary School

January 28, 1984

Dear Mom,

Received your letter of January 3 about a week ago. I hope by now you are getting some warm days and that the snow is melting. Most of the boys are here now and school is going full swing. Many come around to look over all the work that was done during the vacation. The boys are quite amazed that the container project is so far advanced. Even our new regional superior brought one of the new lay missionaries here last week to see the container project. There are quite a few containers around and people are looking for ideas on how to use them.

This past week we have been busy after school selling soap, notebooks, T shirts and pens to the students at a very modest price. All this stuff came in the container last September, but I was saving it for the new school year. We used one of the containers as a store which keeps the boys away from my house. Last year in their anxiety to get things being sold, they trampled on my flowers and broke the front door. You know how things go when there are shortages and people want things.

We have had a lull in the rains this past week, but everything is still very green. We all hope the rains keep coming, but in this country where drought is so persistent, one never knows.

I found a nice young man to help me with the laundry and house work. He comes in 2 mornings a week. I do all my own cooking though, which I prefer. I haven't had many guests lately, at least for overnight, although many stop in here for an hour or two.

I will mail this in the Diamond Mines today. Since their plane goes to Dar 3 times a week now, perhaps the mail will go a little faster.

Much love,
Fr. Marv

Shinyanga Secondary School

April 10, 1984

Dear Mom,

Your nice letter of March 22 arrived a couple of days ago. It is a good idea to send Easter greetings early. Mine will be late I'm sure. I won't be able to get out my newsletter until after Easter. There are always so many things that have to be done... The Mwadui Mines' plane will not be flying for a couple of weeks since it went to Dar es Salaam for service, so you may not get this letter until the end of the month.

This past month my spare time has been taken up writing a theological position paper which will represent our men in Shinyanga and perhaps the whole region if approved for the General Chapter to be held at Maryknoll, N.Y. beginning at the end of September. I feel that what we have to say is very important and so it was worth all the time and effort.

The long rains which were supposed to begin March 15 just didn't come. The pattern seems to be very much like last year's. We have had a few light showers but not enough to sustain crop production and growth. The prime minister of the country, Mr. Sokoini, was at Mwadui Mines a couple of weeks ago. He flew around the area in a helicopter to survey the crop damage. The corn crop is all burned off. The people may get some sweet potatoes, peanuts and millet, but not enough to last very long.

I guess I mentioned the stray dog whom I call "Yatima" (which means orphan in Kiswahili) who was pregnant by my dog, Raha. Yatima gave birth to 8 pups on March 15th. But three were born dead and others seemly died of disease. There is still one left who is well and peppy and beginning to run around, much to the consternation of the mother who is trying to keep her in check. Perhaps this last one will survive.

This Friday Fr. Dick Hochwalt is coming to help me with a communal penance service which will be followed by Stations of the Cross. It seems like Lent just started, but it is practically over.

On Saturday there is graduation for the form 6 class. The blind boys are practicing right now in their container club house. Their nicely done songs will be part of the celebration. After graduation, classes will cease for the form 6 boys, but they will have plenty to do preparing for their final exams which take place in about a month's time. This is how it works out here. Graduation comes before exams so that it is out of the way and there is nothing to interfere with their studies. I guess it makes sense.

I received the art supplies which St. Leonarda sent, which came by container; and also the pictures which came by post. I was really delighted to get everything. Ed Wortman also sent a box of tobacco and candy etc. which was in the container.

I hope you had a great Easter...Happy resurrection season.
My love and greetings to you and all....
Fr. Marv

Dar es Salaam

July 2, 1984

Dear Mom,

I just wrote a few lines to Dorothy and Deb and want to write to you before leaving Dar es Salaam. It has been a very short stay, but I have packed in a lot in the few days that I have been here. John Lange was here for supper one night so I got a chance to see him. Yesterday I visited some of my Goan friends and had a home mass for them because it was the feast of the Sacred Heart. In the afternoon I visited the Youth Center which I had founded a few years ago. They are building a big gymnasium over the tennis court I had put in. When it is finished, the youth will be able to play sports in any kind of weather. The priests in charge now are the Salesians from India. I also had a visit with Fr. George Smith, a White Father who was my co-worker while I was here in

Dar. He is now in charge of the religious education program in all the Secondary Schools in the city of Dar es Salaam. It is nice to see how things have gone on since I left 3 years ago. Tomorrow I head back to Shinyanga. Am booked on a 737 Boeing from Dar to Mwanza. In Mwanza I picked up a connecting flight on an 18 seater Two engine Otter which flies to Shinyanga which is 90 miles away. It would have been easier to take the Mwadui Diamond's plane, but that has been out of order for some time..

School starts on July 9th. Hope you are having a good summer.

Much love,
Fr. Marv

Footnote:

I left Dar es Salaam in 1981 to attend studies in Rome. Fr. George Smith of the White Fathers took over the directorship of the Youth Center in my place. He only had this job for a few months. Cardinal Rugambwa turned the youth center over to the Silesians (Community of Don Bosco), missionaries from India.

St. Paul the Apostle Center
Shinyanga Secondary School,
P.O. Box 57. Mwadui Diamonds Mines, Tanzania

Sunday, July 22, 1984

Dear Mom,

Since I got back from Dar, I haven't had a chance to write, so want to get off a few lines today to tell you how things are going. School is well underway now and I am back teaching in the classroom. We got a slow start because so many of the students arrived late. The first week there were no classes at all. Transport is a big problem, but also many of the students don't start out early enough, something which the headmaster is very concerned about and has plans to correct this next semester.

We have had several meetings of the famine committee. Four containers full of foodstuffs have arrived at Mwadui Diamond Mines, and have been offloaded from the rail cars. The containers were sent by "Mother Theresa's workers" in Canada. It is now our job to see that everything is distributed properly to the various parishes. We will begin this week with two 7 ton trucks, one belonging to the diocese and other to Maryknoll Father, Herb Gappa. I have 60 names representing 60 families who live in the village of Utemeni, all very hard up for food. I will do what I can with the help of the village elders. What we have so far is not very much when we think of the number of people needing help. But we expect much larger consignments later from Catholic Relief services in Dar es Salaam. They expect big shipments from the U.S. department called USAID. Which hopefully will be arriving soon.

I hope that all goes well in Minnesota.
Much love,
Fr Marv

Footnote:

Tanzania in 1984 was experiencing the worst famine it had had in many years. The long rains that ordinarily come in March, April and part of May, did not materialize. The people, for the most part, neglected to plant millet which is much more drought resistant than corn. They much prefer eating corn to millet, but nevertheless each household should have put in an acre or so of millet as insurance. People from the neighboring village gathered around my house daily begging for food. I asked them to go to the government headquarters and ask for grain which was beginning to arrive from donor nations. They refused saying they had tried and received nothing. The 4 containers that came were sent by Mother Theresa's helpers in Canada. Children who had helped pack the containers, had notes plastered on the inside walls of the containers saying how much they loved the people of Africa.

Footnote:

The above is a copy of the letter I sent out to my friends and benefactors, Sept. 1, 1984. It tells the story of the severe drought which was by far the greatest I experienced in my over 30 years in Tanzania. Without foreign help, thousands of people would have died of starvation.

Those in power were selling the donated grain etc. and getting rich. What eventually saved the people was the bulgur wheat which was donated by the United States and distributed by Catholic Relief Services through the Catholic Church. Tons of food were transported by truck all over the country. We church people were all volunteers, donating our time and energy to save the people.

You will notice at the top of this page - "St. Paul the Apostle Center". With the Bishop's permission I had changed the name from "Chaplain's Center" to "St. Paul the Apostle Center" because of my love for St. Paul.

St. Paul the Apostle Center

Nov. 15, 1984

Dear Mom,

Since my last letter the outlook regarding the famine situation here in Shinyanga area has improved. Foodstuffs such as bulgur wheat, and soya flour have begun to arrive in huge trucks, each pulling a wagon which doubles their load. It is a long trek from Dar es Salaam to Shinyanga, about 600 miles, and the road is rough for the last 200 miles. One of the trucks had to abandon its wagon a hundred miles back because of a broken axle. After unloading, the crew went back for the foodstuffs in the wagon. For the most part, however, the trucks are arriving safely.

The U.S. government and C.R.S. deserve high marks for their efforts to help our starving people. The ambassador, John Shirley, was here a couple of months ago to survey the famine problem personally. U.S.A.I.D. which has an office in Dar es Salaam, is the agency of the U.S. Government which

---

after careful survey orders the foodstuffs from the U.S. They hand over the food to Catholic Relief Services which in turn sends it to us. Everything is paid for by the U.S. government including the transport from Dar es Salaam to here which is very expensive, coming to something like $10,000 per load. To see the good that is being done makes one proud to be an American.

The big thing now is to keep the people alive until they can harvest something. The Catholic Church in Germany is contributing 2000 tons of sorghum seed which needs a minimum of rainfall. More is coming from C.R. S. Some of the seed has arrived. I have received 3 bags which I have distributed to the neighboring village of Utemeni . The short rains have begun early this year and many black clouds are approaching. A welcome sight indeed. If all goes well, there should be some sort of harvest by med-February.

People, especially women and children, come to my door every day asking for food. One little old lady said she had not eaten for 3 days which is typical. I could only give her some pudding, all that was left from what we received from the do-workers of Mother Theresa in Canada. My allotment of C.R.S. food has not yet arrived.

As Christmas approaches we are reminded that SGod sent his Son, Jesus, born in poverty to enrich us all with his life which will never end. Jesus calls us to repentance, faith in his life and promises, and love of neighbor. The famine problem, although tragic in its consequences, gives us an *opportunity to respond to that love and can serve to bring the world community closer together.*

May the Lord, the source of all good, bless you during this Christmas season, and every day in the New Year.

The above was my Christmas letter for 1984. The problem of the famine was not totally solved, but at least we were coping. I had men from the village working for me digging a pit for an outdoor toilet. They didn't accomplish much because they had little energy, but I think it was important to have them do something for their wages in food.

Love and prayers,
Fr. Marvin

Footnote:

The picture about the famine changed drastically. The rains started to come in abundance. Even though the people had little to eat and were dependent upon the bulgur wheat shipments, they were filled with hope. If the rains continued, they would have an early harvest and the famine would be over. In planting, the people went back to their traditions and planted drought resistant millet. The government passed a law stating that every farmer had to plant at least 1 acre of millet, although planting corn was not disallowed.

What happened seemed to be a divine intervention. I was listening to radio Tanzania and heard the forecast. No rain was expected and the weather forecast for the future was bleak indeed. It was predicted that according to the meteorological conditions, the chance for a good harvest was very slim.

Interestingly, an American representing USAID, came to see me and to survey the area. He too knew the weather prediction and was helping make plans for continued shipment of bulgur. While we were talking black clouds suddenly appeared and we had a terrific downpour. He also said that if 75% of the food got to the right people (and not ripped off by graft), it was considered a great success. He said that this had been accomplished through the distribution by the churches. We were all very proud of our role in feeding the people.

St. Paul the Apostle Center

Sunday, Jan. 13th, 1985
Feast of the Baptism of the Lord

Dear Mom,

Since I last wrote I have been to Musoma and back (round trip 500 miles) for the regional meeting. My original plan was to drive to Mwanza (90 miles), pick up John Lange, and proceed to Musoma, all on the same day. But it turned out differently. Fr. Jim Travis came here and stayed overnight and the next day we left together in my VW van for Mwanza. We got about half way when we had some trouble with the van. I hit a high ridge on the road which bent the bar which runs between the 2 front wheels. The bar was forced up against the axel which prevented it from moving up and down freely. After about an hour of trying to pry out the bar without success, we finally figured out a way to do it. I had a chain in the car which we tied on one end to a fence post

---

and hooked the other end around the bar. By backing up the car, the force of the engine was sufficient to straighten out the bar and we were able to proceed.

When we got to Mwanza, John Lange was not there, although a plane had arrived from Dar es Salaam. We went to the Bishop's house which is like a big guest house for traveling priests. I was able by good fortune to get a call through to our house in Dar es Salaam, which was kind of like a minor miracle. John Lange was there and said he couldn't come, nor would the others be coming from Dar because the planes weren't flying regularly and thus there weren't enough seats on the plane to take care of the back-log. Also, John said that Fr. Ken Thesing had arrived from New York and needed to get to the meeting and so John gave up his seat for the next day's plane.

I stayed overnight at the Bishop's guest house and the next morning met Fr. Ken Thesing at the airport. We drove up to Musoma without any further complications. The road is pretty good from Mwanza to Musoma. I was a bit shocked to see how dry it was along the way. In that whole area there had been no rain since the middle of December. This was in contrast to the rains we had in the Shinyanga area.

I enjoyed the meeting. We had sufficient time for socializing and recreation. The Chapter delegates (including Fr. Ken Thesing who had been elected to the general council in N.Y.) gave us a run down on the chapter which was interesting. Yesterday Fr. Jim Travis and I drove back. We had lunch in Mwanza to break up the trip.

The school boys have begun to return, but even though school officially begins tomorrow, there certainly won't be any

classes till toward the end of the week... I hear you had a warm December. No doubt January will be cold...
Much love,
Fr. Marv

St. Paul the Apostle Center
January 28, 1985

Dear Mom,

I am writing this from the Bishop's residence in Shinyanga. I came for a meeting on the famine problem. The situation here and in my area is improving. I was visiting the neighboring village of Maganzo which is about 3 miles from the Secondary School and found that some of the people have begun to harvest millet - the first fruits. By the end of February, all those who planted early will be harvesting millet, which means the emergency situation will be over in our area.

Out where Fathers Jim Travis and Dan Ohmann live, however, the situation is still very serious. The rains were about half of what we got and also the army worms attacked the crops killing most of what came up. They will need food assistance for some time to come.

At school all is going along fine. Mosquito nets, notebooks and pens which I ordered about a year ago through Maryknoll, N.Y have arrived and have been mostly distributed. I hope the mosquito nets help reduce the malaria problem.

I hope this finds you feeling well....Greetings to all...
Much love,
Fr. Marv

Charles Gambaseni with his wife and children. Charles was one of the Catholic teachers at the secondary school. We became good friends. He was very helpful to me.

St. Paul the Apostle Center,
Shinyanga Secondary School
P.O. 157, Mwadui Diamond Mines, Tanzania

Feb. 12, 1985

Dear Mom,

Received your letter of January 18 with Rita's addition about a week ago. Am very happy to hear you are feeling better. I remember you in my prayers every day. The rain continues to come here every few days. Two days ago we had about 2 inches, which is the biggest rain we have had since I came here two and a half years ago. This is not the time of year when the big rains come ordinarily. A few days before that we had an inch, so you can imagine the crops are doing excellent. The people are happy and still planting. Many have begun harvesting the first crop of millet and sorghum and are now trying for a second crop.

Last week I passed out food to about 400 families in the two neighboring villages. A couple of the form 6 students helped with the collection of money. Very little is charged, only 30 shillings which is less than 2 dollars. They receive 50 lbs. of bulgur wheat and a gal. of cooking oil. Can't beat those prices. CRS feels it is better to charge something rather than giving everything away free. This will be my last distribution on a big scale. Practically all will be eating their own food in a couple weeks' time. I am really happy the rains have been good. This famine has taken a lot of my time and now I will be able to do other things which have been sitting on the back burner. The Bishop asked me to be the chair person for the "International Youth Year" for the diocese. I want to send some circulars out to the parishes in the diocese, and now I will have time to do it.

One of our Maryknoll priests, Fr. William Murphy, who has worked in Musoma diocese for 35 years, died of a heart attack a few days ago. Quite a few of the men drove up to Musoma for his funeral which was yesterday morning. Fr. Bill was not quite 70.

Hope your weather is not so cold...
Much love,
Fr. Marv

Footnote:

My mother was having health problems due to old age. She was 86 at the time I wrote the above letter. She had a hard time walking. She had carotid arteries in her neck and had a difficult time sleeping. She was living alone in her own house. My sister Dorothy lived only 6 blocks away and came just about every day to see mom. My twin sister, Marlys, lived in St. Paul, about an hour away by car. She called mom every evening.

In the food distribution to the two neighboring villages, I had the form 6 boys helping me. At first I had the village leaders helping me, but I couldn't trust them. They would try to steal food by putting a sack of bulgur or a few cans of cooking oil aside someplace where I couldn't see it.

March 6, 1985

Dear Mom,

Today I received your letter of Feb. 13th and Dorothy's letter of Feb. 14th. Took about 3 weeks. Good to hear you are feeling better. I am very happy to hear that you are getting meals on wheels. Dorothy says it costs only $2.40 per meal which is really cheap.

The rains have continued here. We had almost an inch on March 1. Since the 20th of January we have received 11 inches which is the best January and February I have ever experienced out here. On Monday afternoon I was helping two Red Cross workers give out some food at the town of Maganzo which is about 3 miles from here. Many of the children there have been suffering from malnutrition. We had given out food there about 3 weeks ago. Lisbeth, the Danish nurse had weighed each child. In weighing them again, more than half had gained enough weight to be considered normal which shows that the general picture here has greatly improved. The village chairman at Maganzo said that he has been living in this area since 1958 and has never seen a better crop for this time of year. I believe it is an answer to our many prayers. The rain has been concentrating in the driest areas, the areas most hit by the famine. Other areas only 75 miles from here which were not as bad off, did not receive such good rains as we did. That is too much to be just a coincidence.

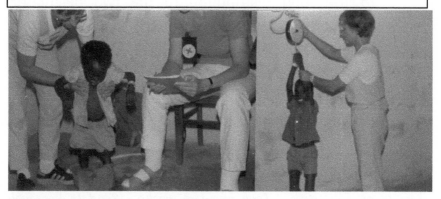

Pictured above: Lisbeth, the Danish Red Cross nurse who was one of the food distributors and health workers in our area. She weighed the children in the town of Maganzo during the famine and then a few weeks later. It was quite remarkable how much weight they gained. Also, the hair color of the children changed. When suffering from malnutrition, the hair turns into a reddish color.

St. Paul the Apostle Center
March 16, 1985

Dear Mom,

There has been no rain for two weeks now, but that is not so important since the people are now harvesting their crops. Many are hoping for a second harvest at the end of May. To accomplish that we will need a lot more rain. I am happy that people are now able to feed themselves. That is the greatest blessing of all. Tomorrow, the 4th Sunday of Lent which is already more than half over. In two months' time, I will be heading for home. The time is going very quickly.

All is fine here at the secondary school. I have been taking a few pictures of the youth so I will have something new to show when I come home. In a few days' time I expect to get out my Easter Newsletter. But I want to send you this special note to wish you a very happy Easter which is the feast of Hope and joy in life eternal as promised by Jesus. When we think that some day we will all be united in the kingdom of God in perfect happiness forever and ever, it makes our troubles here seem quite unimportant.

I am praying for your good health every day and I am really looking forward to seeing you

Much love, Mom today and always. Also many thanks for the Valentine's greeting.
Your Son, Fr. Marv

April 11, 1985
Dear Mom,
A few lines to tell you that I received your nice letters of March 2nd and 18th. I am very happy to hear that you are feeling better. I hope your legs get stronger as the summer approaches.

There is no school this week since it is the mid-term break. It is nice to have it, the week right after Easter. We had a very good Holy Week and Easter Sunday. We had many of the Young Christian Students from Shinyanga Town here as guests during the last three days of Holy Week for what we call "the Easter Conference", which is something like a retreat. On Holy Saturday evening at the Paschal vigil service, I baptized 17 students and 3 babies. The babies are children of the teachers and staff workers. It was a very joyful celebration.

This week I am catching up on my correspondence and getting some rest. Fr. John Lange surprised me by showing up yesterday via the Mwadui Mines' plane. He is here for a Maryknoll meeting which begins next week at Wila parish about 15 miles from here. It has been quite a while since I have seen him since he was not able to attend our regional meeting last January. He looks good.

I am making plans for my home leave. I want to leave the school on May 15th and take the Mwadui Mines' plane to Dar es Salaam. I plan to stop there for just a day and then fly to Nairobi where I will spend a few days working with Fr. Dick Quinn on editing the video tape he took at my place about 6 weeks ago. I want to shorten it to a half hour show which will be nice to show when I get home. I hope to leave Nairobi around May 21 and thus be home about May 23 or so. Best wishes to all...Keep well.

Love and prayers,

Fr. Marv

Footnote:

One of the most important aspects of evangelization is to bring in new members. It was hard work to prepare the students for baptism. Besides my religion classes, I had a special class every Sunday after mass for those preparing for Baptism. It was a day of rejoicing to have 17 converts at Easter of 1985.

In the summer of 1985, I went home for 3 months leave. I had finished 3 years as chaplain of Shinyanga Secondary School. I spent much of the summer gathering things needed and preparing the shipment of a container.

Footnote:

When I went home on leave in the summer of 1985, as usual I stayed with my mother in Minneapolis, Minnesota. I spent much of my time collecting materials for a container shipment to Africa. I stored many things in my mother's garage before bringing them to New Holstein, Wisconsin where they would be put into a container by Brother Regis and his crew. Brother Regis, a Salvatorian, was an expert in preparing containers for shipment all over the world. He had a huge warehouse filled with all kinds of good things collected from donors who could not sell their products but did not want to give them away in the U.S. which would take away from their sales.

The top picture includes myself, my sister, Dorothy, my aunt, Sr. Hugonia and my mother.

The bottom picture is of my aunt, Sr. Leonarda, and my sister, Dorothy. The sisters, Benedictines from Yankton, South Dakota, were visiting. They all enjoyed helping me prepare the shipment. This was the last time I was to see my mother (87 years old at the time) who died on Feb. 3rd, 1986.

St. Paul the Apostle Center
Shinyanga Secondary School

August 19, 1985

Dear Mom,

A week has gone by since I left Minneapolis. This is my first letter since returning to Tanzania. Perhaps I can expand a little from our telephone conversation last Friday....In Amsterdam while waiting for the call to board the plane for Dar es Salaam; I was surprised to meet Fr. Don Lamore, a diocesan priest from Nebraska who worked in Musoma diocese for 5 years. Fr. Don has been back in Nebraska for 3 years and once again has permission from his Bishop for another 5 year hitch in Tanzania. It was nice to have company on the plane. Since the plane was not that crowded, we were able to sit together for part of the time. After a one hour stop in Athens and again in Khartoum, we finally arrived in Dar es Salaam at 2 AM Thursday morning right on time. Fr. John Lange was there to meet us which I did not expect. I got all my bags through customs without any trouble except the box of video cassette tapes. The custom's man made me open it and after examining the contents said I had to pay 1200 dollars duty which is three times the actual cost. It was either that or leave the tapes behind in lock-up until I could get a letter from the ministry of education allowing them in duty free. I chose the latter course. After that, John Lange took us to the Maryknoll house. It looked like it might be difficult and time consuming to get the letter, but as it turned out, John thought of an old friend who works for the ministry of education. More amazingly, this fellow, Mr. Mbaga, turned out to be the first assistant to the principal secretary who is actually the one who writes these letters. Thus the problem was solved. I was able to get the letter the next night. Mr. Mbaga brought it with him to his home after finishing work. I went right down to the customs official at the airport to get the tapes. They then wanted a second letter from the treasury, but after some discussion I was able to procure them without cost, and without a second letter.

The diamond mine's plane was supposed to fly on Friday morning, but fortunately for me it was under repair and did not go until Saturday at 11:15 AM. Thus I was able to bring everything with me - all my bags including the tapes, the video cassette recorder and the T.V. set. The VCR and the TV set had arrived from Japan a couple of weeks before and were stored in the Dar Maryknoll house.

The plane trip from Dar to Mwadui diamond mines takes about 2 and a half hours. There were only 6 passengers. The rest were supplies for the mines plus my stuff. The supplies took 3/4 of the space and were tied down with ropes. The seats are removable to allow for either passengers or cargo...When we arrived I could see Fr. Charles Callahan waiting for me below. After we landed and everything was unloaded, Charlie drove me to the head office where my V.W. Van was being stored. I turned the starter over a couple of times. The battery was still strong and the van started right up, thus winning my bet with Charlie who was convinced that it would not start. We returned to the airport and loaded up my stuff. By this time it was about 2:30 PM. We then drove to the Diamond Mines restaurant where Peter, the chef in charge, was waiting. He had saved some food left over from the noonday meal - liver, spinach and potatoes. That was a nice welcome back. Peter also gave me a couple of loaves of bread to tide me over until I have time to make some...

On the road back to my place, I met Mr. Gedi who had been the watchman here the last couple of months, sleeping in the container house at night. He said everything was O.K. - nothing stolen. The only problem was my two dogs who took off about a month ago. Although they were seen in the vicinity a few times, he had no idea where they might now be.

Sunday morning at the regular time, 9 AM, we had the mass of the Assumption. There was a good crowd. The singing was strong and enthusiastic. After mass I talked with some of the ladies from the neighboring village of Utemeni who jubilantly reported that they have plenty of sweet potatoes and millet to last till the next harvest. That was good news.

Sunday evening I visited Mr. Masaki, the head master, who informed me of more improvements underway at the school such as new benches and light fixtures in the classrooms which had been stolen some years ago.

That brings us to today, Monday. This morning when I got up I heard some whimpering at the door. My two dogs had returned and sure seemed glad to see me. After greeting me the way dogs do, jumping all over the place, their attention was averted by a stray cat, half wild, who also seems to want to make this place her home. I had heard her last night as well as a couple of kittens who evidently are living in the drain pipe underneath the sidewalk between my house and the church.

At 11 AM this morning I went to the staff room for the coffee break and to say hello to all the teachers. At 11:30 I returned home to find my 60 form I students waiting outside the library for their first religion class this term. So you see I am back in the saddle.

I forgot to mention - Fr. Jim Lenihan from the neighboring mission of Wila, came this morning while I was still eating breakfast. Jim brought my video cassettes which had been prepared by Fr. Dick Quinn in Nairobi, for catechetical work. It will take a while to get the video business set up, but at least everything I need is here which is a nice feeling.

That brings us up to date. The time is 4 PM. The temperature is 80 degrees and the humidity 55%. This is the dry season. The countryside is brown and dusty, but not to worry. There is enough food in the storage bins to last until the next harvest which we hope comes again next year. We have to trust in that.

Bye for now...Hope all goes well with you...Greetings to all...

Much love...

Fr. Marv

P.S. Please tell Dorothy I have the green tabernacle veil she made on the tabernacle. It fits perfectly.

Footnote:

The diamond mine's plane was an old DC3, one of the most reliable planes ever built. Later they got a new turbo prop plane which seemed to be always in repair.

The repairs at the school were making things better for the students. I bought 100 folding chairs for the school which would be arriving in a couple o f months in the container which also would be a big help.

Shinyanga Secondary School

September 4, 198.

Dear Mom,

I am back about two and a half weeks now although it seems like a lot longer. I am well established and am teaching regularly. Have had several Maryknollers staying overnight. They like the video very much and I can see in the future there will be many coming. I don't have the video set up in the library yet for the students. We have graduation for the form 4's here on Oct. 12th which will include an open house which means the various departments of the school will have displays for the invited guests to see. I was asked this morning if I would show the video program of St. Paul the Apostle Center. It will be a good way to initiate the video for the students.

I have been doing some baking, made bread, a pie and a cake. I don't have any more cake mix so used an old fashioned recipe for chocolate cake which turned out pretty good. I have quite a bit of dairy whip powder which when whipped up with milk makes a nice topping.

My neighbor, Fr. Charles Callahan at Mwadui Mines, started to have chest pains about a week ago. He has been confined to Mwadui hospital for tests. They found out that

---

he has angina which is a problem of circulation of the arteries which lead to the heart. He is feeling o.k. now but will be leaving soon for the U.S. for further tests. Perhaps he has something like Floyd had and will need a by-pass operation. Fr. Charles is 64 years old and up to now has had very little sickness.

I received my first letter from the U.S. yesterday since arriving back - from Jean Guimont. Letters take about that long as no doubt more will now be coming.

Not much else is new. Yesterday the boys helped me get some sand from the river bed nearby. We want to start making cement blocks for the outdoor toilet.

Hope all goes well. Greetings to all....
Much love,
Fr. Marv

Footnote:

Tanzania did not have a T.V. station until the 1990's. What I introduced at the Secondary school was video. I imported two Video TV's in the container, a large one for the library and a smaller one for my guest room. With the video cassettes I had brought, I had lots of material for teaching religion as well as some very nice recreational movies.

Fr. Charles Callahan was sent to Nairobi for further tests. He did not need bypass surgery, but was put on medications. He was able to continue as chaplain of the diamond mines for 7 more years. He did not die of heart failure, but of cancer. He died in 1994, age 74 and was buried in the small cemetery behind the new Cathedral in Shinyanga town.

Left: During Holy week we had a retreat for the Young Christian Students' organization at Shinyanga Secondary School. Since space was limited, especially for girls, we had to limit the retreat to just a few outsiders from Shinyanga town. The picture is of myself with some of the Young Christian Students.

Right: The imported folding chairs which came in the container from the U.S. The English volunteer, Dave Ecklund is painting the name of the school on the chairs for security sake.

Left: Father Charles Callahan in a typical pose. He always seemed happy and light hearted
Right: The sanctuary and altar of our chapel during lent - Note Tanzanian flag on the right

Footnote:

The Young Christian Students' organization was very well established in Tanzania. It was very effective and the best vehicle we had to bring Christ to the students. They met frequently and discussed the scriptures and tried to relate them to their daily lives. I thought it was the best effort we made to counteract the problem of promiscuity leading to the AIDS crisis.

Left: My good friend, Fr. Richard Hochwalt looking at the camera. We called him "Hocky". He had a doctorate in canon law, taught for a few years before coming to Africa with my group in 1957. Fr. Dick dedicated his whole life to Africa until his death in 2005.
Right: Myself, Fr. Dan Ohmann and Fr. Bill Hofferman

Left: People from the neighboring village of Utemeni who attended mass on Sunday's at the School chapel
Right: Myself with some of our students

Left: A couple from the town of Utemeni
Right: One of the teachers (on the left) painted the stations of the cross which we hung in the chapel

St. Paul the Apostle Center
Shinyanga Secondary School

Oct. 17, 1985

Dear Mom,

Last Saturday was graduation for the form IV students and open house. Each department of the school had a display for the invited guests which were very many. For my part, I showed the video tape of the role of the chaplain with the students of the secondary school which Fr. Dick Quinn had made it earlier in the year. I showed the video in our library about 5 times to at least 70 people each time. It was very popular.

Later on in the afternoon on the same day, Fr. Jim Lenihan brought Fr. Jack Corcoran, the Vicar General of Maryknoll stationed in N.Y., to my place. Fr. Jack is on visitation and is spending about a day at each mission. He stayed overnight participating in the mass on Sunday. After lunch I took him to Wila parish. I stayed there overnight and came back early Monday morning.

The video continues to be a big hit here. I use it almost daily now. I showed a film of the 6 youth of Medjugorje, Yugoslavia, the ones to whom the Blessed Mother is appearing to daily beginning in 1981. The video shows the youth enraptured as they see the vision of Mary which seems to last about 10 to 15 minutes each evening. There has been a great transformation in the village. The church is jammed with people attending mass and saying the rosary. There are at least 30 priests who come there on weekends to help with confessions in various languages for the ever increasing number of pilgrims. All this is shown on the film. Brother Cyril and Fr. Don Sybertz just got back from home leave and stopped at this village in Yugoslavia on the way back. Fr. Sybertz brought the video film which was made by Fr. Bertoluchi, a charismatic priest from the US, who went there to make the film.

I met with my parish council to discuss, among other things, how we can use the video on weekends for entertainment for the students and teachers. The problem is that there are so many, a total of 700 counting the students and teachers with their families. My library only holds about 90.

We are making progress with the outdoor toilet near the church. The hole we dug is pretty deep. The ground wasn't stiff enough and so the walls partly collapsed. I decided to use reinforcing rods and cement with a form to make them firm. Now they should last a hundred years. The students help me. We work after school hours and during their free time on Saturday morning.

We are still waiting for our first big rain. We have had just a few showers so far, not enough to make an impression. The clouds are forming so maybe this week.... Greetings to all.... love and prayers,

Fr. Marv

The construction of the outdoor toilet. When the walls in the hole partially collapsed, I went into the pit by myself to dig the dirt out. I shoveled into a nest of snakes. I climbed out as quickly as possible and fortunately did not get bit. I had several other close calls with snakes some years before.

Girls from the neighboring village of Utemeni. They liked to be around the boys' school for obvious reasons. They came every Sunday for mass. Some of them were in my convert class. You will notice that they are wearing dresses and not the typical African garb called a shuka (a colorful cloth worn around the body with a matching shawl over the head and shoulders). When the girls in the U.S. abandoned dresses in favor of jeans, many bales of used clothing coming to Africa which included discarded dresses. The African girls loved them. They were very cheap at the market.

Saturday, Nov. 16, 1985

Dear Mom,

I am writing this letter from the Shinyanga town parish. I came here with a few of the students from our school to attend a meeting of the YCS (Young Christian Students). The youth from the other schools around here have not yet arrived even though the meeting was supposed to start a half hour ago. Anyhow, that gives me time to write you a few lines.

This past week we had a total of two and a half inches of rain, so now we can say the rainy season is here. The leaves are coming out on the trees and the grass is beginning to come up. The best thing is that now I have water in my tank and don't have to carry it from the tap outside. The tank feeds the bathroom and also the kitchen sink.

Guests have been coming to my place in great numbers. This past week there was someone every day except one. I enjoy the company. After supper the guests like to watch the video which is a nice break.

The form IVs left this morning for home. The school year is already beginning to wind down. The containers have not yet arrived. Last week I was going to fly to Dar es Salaam on the Diamond Mine's plane, but the plane was grounded. It seems that while the fumigators were spraying the engine, they used the wrong mixture which ruined some of the electrical wires. I hear that it will be running again in about a week and so I may still be able to fly to Dar to see what happened to the containers.

I hope that all is well and that you are feeling good.
Much love,
Fr. Marv

St. Paul the Apostle Center

Dec. 6, 1985,   St. Nicholas

Dear Mom,

Almost 4 months have passed since I returned from home leave in the U.S. and resumed my teaching and chaplaincy work here in Shinyanga Secondary School. The school year is now over. The students left yesterday for 6 weeks' vacation. This past term has been a good experience. Improvements in the school have helped morale. For example, with electrical repairs made in the classrooms, there is a place for all to study in the evening. On my part, the introduction of video cassettes for the teaching of religion has done a lot to popularize the subject. Since T.V. does not exist in the country, for most of the students, it was a first. Also the rains have been good so far with a total of 6 inches in Nov. and already an inch these first few days in Dec. People in the surrounding countryside are busy plowing with their oxen and planting their seeds. The country is plagued with shortages of all kinds, but at least the specter of famine is not an immediate threat like it was last year.

Yesterday a half dozen of us Maryknollers made an Advent recollection day at the neighboring mission of Wila. As I listened to that haunting melody, "O come, O come Emmanuel", by thoughts turned to probe into the meaning of Christmas and to ask why above all other times in the year, it is such a joy filled time when our hearts are filled with such a restful peace with good feelings for all. I would like to share with you the fruits of this meditation: "Joy is a natural human response to the presence of the good." (We learned this in Philosophy) Christmas is a living reminder that the greatest good that exists or will ever exist has been offered to us by our Heavenly Father, the gift of Jesus, his only begotten son, born of the Virgin Mary. All we have to do is to say yes to Him and he is ours forever without limit, without termination, without destruction. Thus, since Jesus is the greatest possible good, to have him living within us must necessarily be the source of our greatest possible joy even here on earth. In the year 1513, Fra Giovanni wrote a beautiful meditative poem that speaks of the inner reality of Christmas joy:

"There is nothing I can give you which you have not; but there is much that, while I cannot give, you can take. No heaven can come to us unless our hearts find rest in it today.

No peace lies in the future is not hidden in the present instant. Take peace.

The gloom of the world is but a shadow; behind it, yet within reach is JOY. Take joy.

And so, at this Christmas time, I greet you with the prayer that for you now and forever, the day breaks and the shadows flee away."

I wish you all the joys of this blessed Season, and want you to know that you will be remembered in my Christmas masses. May the joy which is the meaning of Christmas, be with you throughout the New Year. You are in my heart and in my prayers this holy season,

much love.....

Fr. Marv

St. Paul the Apostle Center
Shinyanga secondary School

Dec. 20th 1985

Dear Mom,

Just got your letter on Dec. 4th today. Sounds like you are having another old fashioned winter with so much snow and cold weather. Here the rains are continuing nicely. We had 6 inches of rain in November and so far this month 5 inches. The people are not working as hard as last year or planting as much, but those who do should get a nice crop.

Johnny Paulo, my painter friend from Sayusayu, has been here about 2 weeks now. The church is all finished. I am waiting for one color which I expect Brother John Wohead to bring from Shinyanga. He said he would also bring a long extension ladder. The very high places cannot be reached with my 14 footer. Johnny is working in the living room right now.

I think all the painting will be finished in a few days after Christmas.

Our containers still have not arrived. The problem seems to be negotiating a price with the transporter. It is difficult for Fr. Jim Travis to do this unless he goes to Dar es Salaam personally. He has been trying to do this via his Arab friend in Shinyanga town who runs the petrol station and has a telephone. Anyhow, I hope that we will have them soon. We still have about 3 weeks to go before school starts, and I have some projects which I cannot do without the tools in the container.

Today the sisters and fathers from Gula and Maswa are here in the library watching "Gandi" on the video. They brought their own lunch and are having a kind of a video picnic. Brother John should be here later and stay overnight. I continue to get lots of visitors.

My crowd this Christmas should not be real big, but it will be nice to have the church all painted for the feast day. The New Year is close at hand. I wish you all the blessings and good health in the New Year. New Year's greetings to Dorothy, Don, Marlys, Jack and all their families..
Much love,
Fr. Marv

Footnote:

After finishing Kisukuma language studies in early 1958, I was assigned to Sayusayu Mission (see book I,

"Letters From Africa"). One of my jobs was procuration which meant I was responsible for buying food and supplies and also making sure our water supply was adequate. Johnny Paul was a tremendous help to me. We put up gutters on the rectory roof and built water tanks to get more rain water. In later years I called on him now and then to come wherever I was stationed to help me. I heard that he died in 2007 when a wall fell on him as he was constructing a house. He was about 70 when he died and in his early 20's when I first met him. My place became very popular because I had a video TV player. I was the only one in the diocese who had one.

January 2, 1986
Dar es Salaam

Dear Mom,

This is my first letter of 1986. I am still at the Dar es Salaam house but will be leaving in a few minutes. I wanted to return by Mwadui plane a few days ago, but the plane needs some repair again. I have Fr. Jim Travis' new pickup which is ready to be brought down to Shinyanga. There is a big petrol shortage in the country, but Fr. John Lange was just here and said if I stop by his place at Kibaha, (about 25 miles from here, he has petrol.

Fr. Jim will be happy to get his new vehicle anyways so maybe it is better that I drive. It is 600 miles and takes 2 days.

The two containers left by train on Dec. 24 and should be at the diamond mines within two weeks at the most.

> *It was great talking to you on the phone. Happy New Year to you and all.*
> *Much Love,*
> *Fr. Marv*

Footnote:

I had a very difficult trip, especially because someone tried to steal the battery out of Fr Jim's vehicle. I stopped at Fr. John Lange's mission to get 5 gals. of gasoline. I also had to get permission from the government to drive on Sunday to get permission to drive on Sunday which was otherwise forbidden. While I was in the building someone tried to steal the battery and was almost successful. When I came out of the building, the hood was up on the pickup. The brackets which hold the battery were missing, as well as all the covers of the battery where you put in the water. I must have surprised the thief by my quick return and he didn't have time to take the battery. Evidently his anger that he couldn't get the battery took over and he removed the covers. I wasn't sure what to do. I had a piece of rope with me and tried to tie the battery down so it wouldn't jump around. The first part of the trip to Dodoma was ok because the road was tarmac. The second part of the trip was terrible because the road was so bad causing the battery to jump around and acid to jump out of the battery, which cut the rope. I had to stop every half hour to retie the battery down. I finally let quite a bit of air out of the tires so the pickup wouldn't jump around so much on the bad road. When I got to Sengida, I stayed overnight at the diocesan guest house. There was a diocesan mechanic there, who found some old covers to put on the battery so at least the rest of the way the acid was not coming out.

The above was the last letter my mother received from me before he passed away. She died sometime during the night of February 3 of a heart attack. She lived in her own home and was able to take care of herself until the end. She never wanted to go into a nursing home and the good Lord granted her wish. She was 87 years old. The last letter she wrote to me was on January 14, 1986. I have copied it below. It is typical of the letters she wrote.

My mother's letter was not easy to read so I typed it out here for convenience:

Jan. 14, 1986

Dear Son, Fr. Marvin,

Your letter of Jan. 2 is here, came yesterday. Dorothy will come over and take care of the check and get it in your account. You are making that 600 mile trip with Fr. Jim's truck. I hope you will make that alright. I hope you will get containers soon.

We have had no new snow for a week now, but just a bit warmer and days getting just a bit lighter. I am feeling pretty good and cozy in my house – not much news this month of January, been very cold. Hope all goes well for the rest of it, Just wonderful to talk to you on the phone.

I heard from my sisters. Al seems O.K. Marlys' tooth is better. She sure had an awful infection in that. I can't see how anything could get so bad. When it broke, matter came out of her nose and everything.
Much love and prayers,
Mom

St. Paul the Apostle Center

January 31, 1986

Dear Mom and Dorothy,

I want to write this letter to both of you since I want to explain about the unloading of the containers which makes us all very happy. Like I explained in a recent letter to Dorothy, the containers arrived by rail at Mwadui Diamond Mines on January 17. Fr. Jim Travis was looking for a big semi to bring the containers fully loaded to his mission. This would have saved some expenses but it didn't work out. A truck so large was not available and also the crane at Mwadui was not up to full strength and could not lift the heavier container weighing 19 tons. But it could lift the lighter one weighing 14 tons. We then unloaded the lighter one from the ground, while the heavier one was unloaded right from the flat car. Since the containers were placed door to door when they were put on in Dar, one container had to be removed before we could get the doors open. The reason they were put door to door was to prevent thieves from breaking in. It took two days to unload. I got all my stuff out the first day. Jim hired 3 trucks for his stuff. He had to come back for a couple of hours the second day to finish the job.

I now have everything pretty much sorted out and in its proper place. My old worker and friend from Sayusayu, Johnny

Paulo, has been here all month and has really been a big help. Many of the things I wanted to do during the school vacation are now done, even though the containers arrived so late. Johnny and I have been putting in some long days this past week to get the jobs done.... The couch is now finished and in its place in the video room. The red upholstery covered foam looks just like it did when Dorothy made it. When first taken out of the box, it had kinks in it, but they all came out after one day.... The two big packing boxes are now made into cabinets, painted and are standing in my hallway fully loaded. I am using the tabernacle veils now according to the color of the feast day... I tried out the xerox machine and it works...Also the sewing machine and it also works just fine. Johnny refinished and varnished the top of the cabinet.... Yesterday we put the new toilet seat in the out-door toilet. Johnny painted the outside of the outhouse a dark brown and so it is ready for use now too.... I tried using the sawzall by cutting the heavy metal siding of the container that is going to be made into a guest house. The door is now in, almost as easy as cutting out paper dolls. Since I am teaching every day now, it will take a little time to finish the guest house, but I expect to have it done before Easter.

I want to thank you both for your letters - mom's written on Jan. 8 and 14, and Dorothy's written on Dec. 8. I hope your weather warms up soon.... It continues to rain nicely here. We had 8 1/2 inches in January - really marvelous....
Much love,
Fr. Marv

Footnote:

Mom's letter on the previous page was the last one she wrote.... The xerox machine was old and out of date. However, I got quite a bit of use out of it. It had ink cartridges that could be filled with black powder which came with it. I bought it for $100.

My mother, of course, did not get the opportunity to read the above letter written on Jan. 31 since she died on Feb. 3. I found out about her death from Brother Cyril. He received a long distance phone call from my brother and drove out to the Secondary school to tell me. He arrived about 8 PM. Fr. Jim Lenihan and I were watching a film in the video room when he arrived. Since our missionaries in Tanzania rarely travel at night, I knew there was something seriously wrong when I saw him. He said, "I am sorry to have to tell you, Fr. Marv, but your mother has passed away."

It took some time before I could get to Dar es Salaam to get a plane for Europe and the U.S. Fortunately the plane from Mwadui Diamond Mines began flying again within a few days and I could get to Dar. I got the first flight out that I could on KLM airlines. I remember it so well because when I got to Amsterdam it was so terribly cold and I didn't have winter clothes to wear. When I finally got to Minneapolis, it was a few days after my mom's funeral. I stayed at her house. My sister, Rita, coming from Arizona, also stayed there. It was a good thing. We could grieve together and share many memories of our childhood days with mom. I stayed home for a couple of weeks. There was a terrific snow storm with a couple of feet of snow. I had not experienced a winter for so many years. It seemed such a stark contrast to the tropical weather I had just left in Tanzania. When I got back to Africa, instead of writing to my mom, I began to write regularly to my older sister, Dorothy, who took over as my correspondent and sort of a second mother. And so the letters and the story continue.

Dar es Salaam

March 3, 1986

Dear Dorothy,

A few words to tell you that I arrived safely in Dar es Salaam. The flight was very nice all the way. The weather in Paris was nice too. The temperature was about 30 degrees, and there was a light snow. The hotel in Paris was cheaper than I expected - only about $30. When I arrived in Dar, 5 AM Saturday morning, I went through customs and immigration in a matter of minutes. It is really fast when you have only carry-on luggage.

This morning I went down to the Diamond Mines office to check on their plane. I am booked for tomorrow's flight (Tues. March 4) so I should be back at the Secondary school by tomorrow afternoon.

My body clock is still not in tune with the time here. I have no trouble sleeping in the afternoon, but have trouble sleeping at night. In a couple of more days I should be back to normal.

I was happy to be home for a couple of weeks. It will take some adjustment for all of us with mom gone, but being home was very helpful to begin that adjustment.

I hope Margaret and John can swing the loan. Let me know how things go.

My best to Deb and every one.
Love,
Fr. Marvin

Footnote:

Dorothy's daughter and her husband, John, wanted to buy Mom's house. They were working on a loan.

Footnote:

Another 12 boys were chosen for Baptism which took place at the Easter Vigil. For me this was the greatest satisfaction, fulfilling the mandate of Christ, "God teach all nations".

St. Paul the Apostle Center

Easter Tuesday, April 2, 1986

Dear Dorothy,

Thank you for your letters of March 6 and 11. I have made a note to say the masses for mom asked for by Dick Mars. I see you are progressing going through all the stuff in the house. Like you say, the biggest problem is to know what to do with everything.

I haven't had a chance to write for a while. I had a lot of catching up to do and had to put letters aside. . Besides teaching, I had to question the catechumens to check on their progress. 12 of our lads were chosen for baptism which

164

joyously took place at the Easter Vigil. Holy Week services came off nicely. My sewing machine was a big help with the decorating. Fr. Tom Shea had gotten me four 12 ft. lengths of design material from Nairobi which I hemmed and hung like tapestries. The chapel is beautiful now with the new paint job and all the decorations. Five Maryknollers came here for Easter Monday. They watched "St.Thomas Becket" on video. I cooked them a big supper with roast pork, baked potatoes, eggplant, salad and chocolate cake.

Although the month of Feb. was rather poor for rain, the overall average for this growing season has been good. Since Nov. 1, we have had a total of 28 inches so far. I expect we will get another 4 or 5 this month, the last month of the rains. Since 30 inches is considered a good year, we are doing o.k. There is no talk of famine although several areas are not so good. Ed Wortman gave me a rain gauge which I have on the roof of the container which gives me a very accurate picture of the rainfall. There is no school this week and most of next. There are 400 guest students on campus right now from various schools within a range of 50 miles. They are here for a sports week which consists mostly of soccer and track. Our own boys who are not in sports were asked to go home during this period to make room for the guests. I showed some of the guests the video of the '84 Olympics last Sunday night (Easter). Other than that my place is quiet. I have all kinds of little projects to do. I don't have my new curtains up yet, but slowly the place is looking nicer. I planted some flower seeds I had gotten from Virgil

Welna around the statue of St. Francis out in front. It's fun to do these things when you have a little leisure.

I hope the snow has melted now and the weather is more comfortable. I haven't made a decision about coming home in June yet. But if there is enough to do to set up a container, I will come. I saw the regional superior about getting 2 way radio sets for our missions. He is very interested and will be here next week with the final word.

Hi to everyone. Glad to hear that Marlys and Floyd finished the painting on their house. Bet it looks nice.
Love and prayers,
Fr. Marvin

Footnote:
The reason for the radio sets was because we had no communication between our mission parishes. We had to get permission from the government to set up radios. They would only agree if the radios were low power. I was delighted to baptize 12 of our students at Easter. This was the greatest missionary satisfaction following Christ's mandate – Go teach all nations.

St. Paul the Apostle Center
Tuesday, July 8, 1986
Dear Dorothy,
Before leaving Dar. I dropped you a short note. This letter takes up from there. The two doctors, Bill Freida and

Richard Kirsch, and I drove in their new land rover on Friday, July 4, 300 miles to Dodoma. The road is Tarmac all the way which is no strain. We stopped about half way at Morogoro to visit the excellent market there and picked up some fruit and vegetables. I even got a couple of loaves of bread which is almost unheard of these days. We arrived in the evening about 5:30 at Dodoma. The diocesan guest house where I usually stay was filled up. The sisters in the area were having a meeting. A young African priest suggested we go to the Passionist's Fathers center house about 6 miles outside of town, which we did. They have a neat place with quite a few guest rooms and gave us a nice welcome. They had recently put in radio communications so it was helpful to me to hear about the difficulties they had in getting permission from the government.

The next morning we left about 6 A.M. about 15 minutes before sunrise since we had a long ride ahead of us on a very rough road. All went well. We switched off driving and arrived at my place at 5:30 P.M. It was interesting to see how much progress had been made by TANESCO (the Tanzania electric company) in putting up the huge towers which will bring electricity to this area from the hydro-electric dam at Kidato (In the southern part of the country near the Mozambique border) Since the end of May the workers have advanced 30 miles. They said they expect to reach Shinyanga town by the end of August which means that Shinyanga may have a constant flow of electricity by the end of the year. (Diesel generators are being used now which are very irregular)

The two doctors left me off and drove the land rover to Shinyanga. Everything was fine at my place. With no rain for over a month, there is a noticeable change in the landscape. Leaves have fallen and the grass has turned brown. Sunday morning I had mass as usual. Very few students have returned. The next day, Monday, was a national holiday like our independence day. Fr. Jim Lenihan was sitting on my stoop waiting to get in. He stayed overnight and brought me an update on the latest happenings in the diocese.

(From other side of letter) - That brings us up to date. I want to work on the container today. I am trying to get the paneling in and the place set up as a guest house before school starts in a few days...The weather here is very cool these days. This morning it was 50 degrees, the coolest I have ever experienced here.

Greetings to Deb and all,

Love and prayers,

Fr. Marvin

Footnote:

Communication was very difficult between our mission stations. I had suggested that we try setting up ham radios at each mission. The Italian missionaries in Dodoma had succeeded in getting permission from the government and installed the ham radios in their diocese. To get permissions from the government was quite a hassle.

How things have changed in 20 years. Today cell phones are super abundant. Radio communication is out of date.

The European Union sponsored the electrification project for Tanzania. They built a dam on the Ruaha river which was in the South Eastern side of the country. The hydro-electric scheme, even though not perfect, was a marvelous improvement from the diesel generators which produced electricity on a very limited scale.

A word about one of my dogs, Doto, whom I really liked. She was one of the descendants of Raha, whom I had brought with me from Dar es Salaam. I had to have Raha put to sleep by the vet at the Diamond Mines because of VD and blindness. When I went home for my mother's funeral, I had asked Mr. Gedi to guard my place, stay overnight in the container house and also feed Doto. As soon as I left, Doto took off. She ate the leftover food from the student's kitchen which was piled outside. She found a place to have her pups, an old chicken house which was not being used. After the teacher informed me that Doto was there with her pups, I went to the chicken house and found Doto with her pups. She was so happy to see me. She left the pups and followed me home. After I fed her, she returned to her pups. She started coming every evening for food. When she didn't come one evening, I went looking for her. She finally came about 9 PM. I could see she was very sick. She may have been poisoned. She cried all night. I put a blanket over her to keep her warm. The next morning she was dead. I really felt bad. Doto was a great dog. Even when very sick, she still went back to nurse her pups the final night of her life. Fortunately, the pups were old enough to drink from the dish. I went to the chicken house and fetched the 10 pups. I built a small corral for them and began feeding them. They all survived. One of them, Blacky, was to become one of my favorites later on when I was assigned to the youth center in Shinyanga town. That's an interesting story which I will tell later.

St. Paul the Apostle Center
Shinyanga Secondary School

Oct. 16, 1986

Dear Dorothy,

Thanks much for your letter of Sept. 30th. Lots of good things are happening. I am happy to hear that Margaret, John and family are getting settled. I heard from Margaret and also Jack. Seems like everyone is happy about the house deal.

My container arrived 8 AM Oct. 3rd. Since it left New Holstein on July 23, the total time was just over 2 months which must be some sort of a record for swiftness. With the help of some of the students and a teacher, (all members of my parish council), everything was unloaded the same day. The next day the crane from Mwadui Diamond Mines came and lifted the empty container off the truck and on to the foundation prepared for it in the teachers' housing area. Almost everything has been picked up by those who ordered things. The medicines, which was more than half the

---

container, are now in Shinyanga, and Fr. Dan Ohmann was here yesterday to get his small tractor. Tell Don when you see him that the batteries and the acid arrived in perfect condition. Really nice to have everything arrive so quickly, safely and efficiently. The chalice from the Renners was also in the container. It is beautiful.

Last week I was in Musoma for the first regional council meeting. I drove up in my V.W. van, about a 7 hour drive. Gasoline is much easier to get now which makes traveling not so much of a hassle. I was able to buy gas at the pump in Musoma - the first time in 5 years. The meeting was interesting and helpful. Part of the meeting was a workshop to get us off on the right foot. Fr. John Rich (class behind me at Maryknoll) who has expertise in giving leadership workshops, worked with the 4 of us for 3 days giving personality tests, problem solving methods, etc. , so that we could understand and work together better as a team. I have to go back for another meeting in Musoma on Nov. 14th. With this job as a member of the regional council, I will have to do a lot more traveling.

We had 2 inches of rain on Oct. 13th - a cloud burst, the first of the new growing season and a couple of weeks earlier than last year. This is spring time. The leaves are beginning to reappear on the trees. Things are looking good... Greetings to all...

        Much love and prayers,
        Fr. Marvin.

Footnote:

In June I went home again to Minneapolis to work on preparing a container for shipment. Since my mother had died Feb. 3, I now stayed with my sister, Dorothy. I used her garage to store things until I could bring them to New Holstein, Wisconsin where the Salvatorians, Brother Regis and Sister Dora would load up the container and send it to Dar es Salaam. The teachers asked for the empty container which they wanted to use for a small club house. I gave it to them, and also cut out a door and several windows with my sawzall.

I had more meetings to go to than usual. I had been elected to the regional council for a term of 3 years. Fr. Ed Hayes was elected Regional Superior. Fr. John Eyble, myself, and Fr. Herb Gappa, was elected as his assistants.

December 8, 1986

Dear Dorothy,

The school boys have now left, the last one last night, which gives me time now to catch up on many things. I will help the teachers with their container which they will turn into a club house. I have the mass of the Immaculate Conception for the teachers, staff and a few people from the neighboring town of Utemeni at 4 PM today. We are *having wonderful rains. The people are busy plowing and planting.*

I guess this won't get to you in time for Christmas but know that I am thinking of you and hope your Christmas was the greatest. Tell Deb the pups (I still have 3) are over 35 lbs each now and doing great.

Tell John we ran into a problem with the radios. The government said the sets were too powerful and would enable us to listen to army and police calls, so I don't know what will happen. Our Regional superior, Fr. Ed Hayes, went to Dar to try to straighten it out. We are hoping for the best.

A very Merry Christmas and Happy New year...
Much love and prayers,
Fr. Marvin

Footnote:

We had been trying to find a way to help our communication problem for some time. I bought several ham radios second hand while in the U.S. and put them in the container. Now that they were in the country, apparently illegally, we were not sure what to do. How things have changed since those days. Now cell phones are everywhere, including way out in the bush.

Footnote:

The "Mission Forum" publication was very well done. It was about the size of a magazine. Almost everyone wrote something for it. I wrote about my teaching experience at the Secondary School and how important it was not to water down the Faith. I had seen religious textbooks being used in the U.S. which watered down the faith, like teaching that all religions lead to God and therefore are sort of equal; also there was a strong emphasis on social issues and very little about teaching the commandments and the sacraments. The result was a whole generation that grew up without sound doctrine.

St. Paul the Apostle Center

Dec. 29, 1986

Dear Dorothy,

Thanks for your lovely Christmas card. Received it along with several others the day after Christmas. Just so you know, I have received your letters of Nov. 8, 22, and 30. I want to thank the mission group for their generous donation.

Christmas here was very nice. Although the school boys are gone, the group from the neighboring village of Utemeni. is getting bigger and bigger. Many are studying for Baptism. About 10 were baptized in my last class in early November. Also the number of Catholics among the teachers and staff is quite large. Most are coming to mass now. I validated one of the teacher's marriages just before Christmas. We had the midnight mass at 8:30 P.M., early enough so the people from the village would have ample time to walk home which is 3 miles away. On Christmas day we had mass at 9 A.M, attended pretty much by the same people. There is a core of youth from the village, about a dozen girls and a couple of

---

boys between the ages of 16 and 20, who are the mainstay of the choir when the school boys are not here. Several of the girls were just baptized in November.

Yesterday, the feast of the Holy Family, I gave out clothing after mass to these village youth, sort of a reward for all their hard work. There were quite a few new dresses in the last container shipment which were put in by Brother Regis. Everyone found something that would fit. Yesterday afternoon I joined the village youth at one of their homes for a party. A couple hundred were present. We had a meal of chicken and rice. The choir put on a song and dance routine. Different songs from the ones they sing in Church, but with religious themes. They looked terrific decked out in their new clothing. I enjoyed it very much and afterwards invited everyone not yet baptized to join the church. Getting to know these people all began at the time of the famine. Now we are beginning to see the fruits of all the head work there.

The rains continue to be remarkable. It rained 19 days so far this month for a total of 13 inches, probably the most for December since the great rains in 1961 which had broken all the records. The rains are not depressing because there are usually several hours of sunshine every day. If the rains keep up, the crops should be excellent.

Sorry to hear about Sylvia's sudden death. Toni wrote. I have written to Don and Toni. They will miss her a lot...... Enclosed are 4 unsigned checks for my account. I am leaving soon for Shinyanga town and will mail this there. We are having a get-together today for the African and Maryknoll Fathers in the Shinyanga area.

Best wishes for a holy and happy New Year.'
Love and prayers,
Fr. Marvin

Footnote:

My brother Don was married to Toni. I had his wedding shortly after I was ordained in June of 1957. Sylvia was Toni's mother.

Musoma, Tanzania

January 9th, 1987

Dear Dorothy,

Today is Friday. We are finished with our regional assembly here in Musoma. I arrived with 2 other Maryknollers last Saturday morning. Tomorrow we go back to Shinyanga. Every year the trip up here gets a little easier because the new tarmac road continues to progress. It is now finished for about 150 miles, which leaves 100 of dirt road. My Volkswagen is still holding up O.K. I had hoped my new Toyota pickup truck would be here by now. But there was some kind of a mix-up in Japan. I guess the computer punched in the wrong kind of truck, a single cab rather than a double cab, and so it had to be reordered. I guess it will be about May now before it comes in. The sooner the better because I have a lot more traveling to do as you know.

The weather has been really nice. It looks like there may be a shift in the weather for a while.

The meeting went well. The regional council experience has been good for me, gaining new confidence and realizing that I have something to offer.

Will mail this in Mwanza which should shorten the delivery time a couple of days...

Love and prayers,

Fr. Marv

St. Paul the Apostle Center

Saturday, Feb. 28, 1987

Dear Dorothy,

Many thanks for your letter of Jan. 14th and Feb. 4, and the letter from Mrs. Popehn included in your Jan 14th letter. I am writing this from the parish in the town of Shinyanga. We have a meeting here for the Young Christian Students from the various schools around. Since the main post office is nearby I like to mail my letter here. If I send them through the Mwadui Diamonds, the letters still have to come here.

There are new Secondary (High) schools popping up here and there. They are sponsored by the parents with aid from the government. The school where I teach is totally a government school. The new schools don't have as many facilities, of course, but it is an effort to educate more on the high school level. Most do not have anyone to teach religion.

I am trying to get the Young Christian Students' organization started in them so at least there is some contact with the Church.

We have not had rain for two weeks and need it right now. Those who planted their crops early are in good shape and are already harvesting. Most in our area were late. Many do the work by hand with hoes and it just takes them a long time to get the soil prepared.

Hope you are getting good weather with an early Spring. Have a good Lenten season.

Love and prayers,
Fr. Marvin

"Never let anything so fill you with sorrow as to make you forget the joy of the risen Christ." ~ Mother Teresa

St. Paul the Apostle Center,
Shinyanga Secondary School
PO Box 157, Mwadui, Tanzania

March 23, 1987

Dear friends,

Greetings and happy springtime. Since our school is situated smack dab in the middle of farm country, I am very conscious of how the crops are doing and how our neighboring farmers, many of whom pray at our school chapel, are faring. Harvest time is approaching. Although we had excellent rains in Nov. and Dec., they have slowed down considerably since then. Although wise farmers who planted early, have good crops and those who took no chances and put in drought resistant millet, will make out well. Many take chances on corn since it is much less work to harvest and makes better "ugali" (their staple, a boiled flour which they cook until stiff.)

The youth here continue to enter the Church in good numbers. My group of 70 catechumens is about equally divided between the village youth and the boys here at the school. Our Lady's message to the world at Medjugorje, Yugoslavia, has made a big impression here. (I have shown them the video film) Between 70 and 80 boys meet every Saturday night to pray the rosary and meditate on the gospel. There is also a notable increase in the number of confessions and Holy Communions. Mary's prolonged appearances (June 24, 1981 until now) I think, are very significant. They point out the extreme seriousness of our times. Peace will only come about through conversion, prayer and fasting. Mary has also reaffirmed the basic truths of our faith and the importance of the sacrament of confession. I think she is telling us all to hold fast to the things we have always believed in because they are all true.

There will be a number of youth, the members of the Young Christian Students organization, visiting from various schools on Holy Thursday, Good Friday, Holy Saturday and Easter Sunday, very special days for us all.

> *Please be assured of my prayers during this Holy Season. I thank you all for your support and your payers. I wish you Easter joy in Jesus and may our Blessed Mother, the Queen of Peace, guide and protect you always.*
>
> *Peace and Love in the risen Christ,*
> *Fr. Marvin*

(The above – Easter letter to friends and benefactors)

Footnote:

I sent a copy of my Easter newsletter to my sister, Dorothy, and also used it as a birthday card. Her birthday was on March 28. Catherine Scott was a classmate of Dorothy's going way back to the first grade at St. Helena's school in South Minneapolis.... Fr. Richard Duffy and I were classmates at St. Thomas College in 1948-49. He became a Franciscan and worked as a Missionary in Brazil for many years. When they asked for volunteers to go to Africa on the 800th anniversary of the birth of St. Francis, Fr. Duffy volunteered. I never thought that we would be in Africa in the same country. He was working in Bukoba, a city on the Western side of Lake Victoria. He was planning a trip to visit me. I told him I would meet him in Mwanza, on the southern shores of Lake Victoria. He was going to come from Bukoba to Mwanza by boat across the lake.

St. Paul the Apostle Center

May 25, 1987

Dear Dorothy,

I think the last letter I have from you was written on April 26th. No doubt there is one on the way, but I had better not wait for it is about 3 weeks since I have written.

The head master decided to close school early this year because our school is scheduled to hold a sports week for all the schools in the district beginning next week. Last week I gave all my exams and now have them all corrected which was a big job. Most of the boys have already left for home. There is a big problem with transport. A train was derailed which held up train travel for about 3 days. There are very few buses. For those of us who have the money to fly, even that is just about impossible. I understand there is now only one plane able to fly in the whole country because all the planes are in need of spare parts. This is one of the lows in the cycle.

I had to postpone the baptisms at Easter which will now be on Ascension Thursday. There just wasn't time to finish all the lessons. I have been working hard with the catechumens with 3 classes a week. The Bishop is coming to do the Baptisms and at the same time, the confirmations. Since the school closed early, I wasn't able to do anything about that. I could not move up the date for the Bishop because he has a full schedule. There will be a total of 19 baptisms which include a few youth from the neighboring town of Utemeni.

In a previous letter, I mentioned that "Tiny", the smallest dog from my Dog, Doto, who had 10 puppies and was poisoned quite a while ago, gave birth to 5 puppies about 5 weeks ago. They are now 5 weeks old and very lively and eating on their own. I got rid of two yesterday to a couple at the Diamond Mines, and will get rid of the other 3 this week. My other dog, Snoopy", is about to give birth. She dug a big hole in the flower bed in front of my house and is lying in it right now and so I suspect she will give birth today.

I finally heard from Duffy who confirmed that he will be in Mwanza on Pentecost Monday. He will be coming by Lake Steamer on Lake Victoria from Bukoba on the opposite side of the lake. I had a meeting the previous week in Mwanza with the regional council so it should all work out fine. I plan to bring Duffy here for about a week. We can play tennis at the Mwadui diamond mines where there is a good court.

I plan to go to Dar at the end of June to pick my new vehicle (a Toyota double cab pickup). My passport runs out in July, and so I can get that renewed too while I am there. Brother Cyril is driving the 600 miles to Dar and so I can hitch a ride with him.

Hope all goes well. I hope you enjoyed your trip with Joel and Virgil to visit the sisters in Yankton. Hope all is well. .Hi to your daughters Deb and Margaret.....
Love and prayers,
Fr. Marv

Footnote:

In the P.S. I say: "I hope your trip to Yankton with Virgil and Joel works out". Virgil Burns was my classmate at St Thomas College in St. Paul in 1948 and 1949. His wife, Joel, and my sister Dorothy were very good friends. They all went to Yankton, South Dakota, to see my two Benedictine Aunts, Sr. Leonarda and Sr. Hugonia. Virgil will appear again in my life in 1996 and years following. He will have set up a retreat center on a farm in Waconia, Mn. And will invite me to work there after my retirement from my work in Africa.

St. Paul the Apostle Center
Shinyanga Secondary School

June 16, 1987

Dear Dorothy,

I am off to Mwanza today with Fr. Duffy, and will mail this letter there. I picked up Fr. Duffy a little over a week ago after finishing our regional council meeting. Things worked out real good. Duffy was on the Lake Steamer coming from Bukoba which is an 8 hour trip across Lake Victoria. We drove up the hill in the town of Mwanza to Fr. John Eybel's place near Bugando hospital, made a lunch and drove the 90 miles to my place, Shinyanga Secondary School the same evening arriving at 10 P.M.

We have had a real good time together. We said mass together, played tennis, and even did some work. Duffy helped me put in a cement floor in a garage I am building which will have a wood frame and industrial siding imported in a

---

container from the U.S. I hope to have the garage finished by the end of the month. On July 1, I will be driving to Dar with Brother Cyril to get my new Toyota pickup which is now cleared through customs .

Fr. Duffy likes the Tupperware which you sent for him. The time has come for Fr. Duffy to go. We will drive to Mwanza today and get him on the boat to Bukoba which leaves at 8 P.M. Fr. Duffy is also due for home leave to Minneapolis next summer. It looks good for getting together again soon.

Footnote:

Fr, Duffy and I were classmates at St. Thomas College in St Paul, Minnesota. I left for the Maryknoll seminary at the end of my sophomore year. Duffy left a year later for the Franciscans. I had no idea he was going to do this.

Dar es Salaam

July 6, 1987

Dear Dorothy,

I am writing this from our house in Dar es Salaam. Brother Cyril, Fr. Tom Shea and I arrived here from Shinyanga on July 2. It is a two day trip. The first 300 miles is the hardest since it is on a dirt, very rough road. It took us a little over 12 hours to get from my place to Dodoma. At Dodoma we stayed overnight with the Passionists Fathers, an Italian group which has its center house about 9 miles outside of town. The next day to Dar was easy. It is about 300 miles but all tarmac road and took only 6 hours.

When we arrived at the Maryknoll house, I was happy to see my new vehicle sitting in the yard. It was worth waiting for. I don't know if you have seen these double cab pickups. There are not very many in Minneapolis. It has 4 doors and is very easy to get in the front or the back seat. It has a 5 foot box in the back for baggage. When I get time, I may enclose the back and put in removable seats so that I can carry a total of 8 passengers when needed. I can make the shell in the back out of plywood.

Brother Cyril is going on to the United States where he will have an operation for cataract removal on one eye. Fr. Tom Shea and I will be returning to Shinyanga on Wednesday, July 8th which is the day after tomorrow. Like coming, it will take two days. We will probably stay overnight with the Passionists again. With the new car, it should be a bit easier. We would like to take off tomorrow, but I have to wait for my new passport which has taken a little extra time to get ready because of the 4th of July holiday at the embassy. But it is just as well since it gives me a little more leisure and chance to rest. The house looks really nice here. Fr. Tokus has restored it to its original luster. He has had all the buildings repainted on the outside with special paint for the tropics which resists mildew. It is kind of a tan with white trim which looks fresh and attractive. Having put in so much work here, it is nice to see everything kept up. Many of the curtains have been replaced since they don't last so long in the tropics.

It is very possible that this will be my last year at Shinyanga Secondary school. The Bishop would like me to go to the new youth center in Shinyanga town which has been in the process of being built for many years. The delay was caused by contact problems, shortage of materials, etc. Hopefully, the house and library will be ready by next June so that I can move in. Brother Cyril has taken over this part of the construction. The other buildings will need a contractor since there is so much to be done. Right now the project stands about two thirds finished.

I told the Bishop I would agree to go there if he can find someone to take my place at the Secondary School. We have a couple of new priests in the diocese from Ireland. One of them, Fr. Dan Cashman, worked with secondary school students in Nigeria for many years and is very interested in taking my place. He needs the permission of his regional superior who is in Nigeria, but it is fairly certain that he will get the O.K. Thus the plan would be for me to spend one more year at Shinyanga Secondary school and when I return from home leave in 1988, go to the new place which hopefully then will be ready for occupancy. I think I am still young enough to start over again since I had quite a bit of experience, it is not quite like beginning from scratch.

Till next time, love and prayers,

Fr. Marvin

Footnote:

The youth center in Shinyanga town had been started about 5 years previous by Fr. Bill Tokus. An Indian contractor was hired and got the 4 buildings up including the roofs but not much else. He got into trouble with the government and actually spent some time in jail. When he got out, Maryknoll gave him 10,000 dollars more to continue the project. However, he ran off to England with the money thinking that he might be arrested again. Our Superior General, Fr. Boteler, came on visitation and seeing the youth center is in such a sorry state, agreed to give another 150,000 dollars hoping that it could be completed. Youth work was so important. I don't want to get ahead of my story and tell you how it finally reached its completion. It is quite a story. Read on:

As regards the ham radios which we had imported into the country in the container hoping to be able to communicate better, at least between our principal headquarters in Musoma, Shinyanga, and Dar es Salaam, - our regional superior, Fr. Ed Hayes went to Dar es Salaam to see government officials. They gave us permission to use less powerful radios which we then bought. An expert from the company which sold these radios came around and set them up in July of 1987. They worked just fine. The more powerful ones were put in storage. I have no idea what finally happened to them. As of this writing (2009) all radios are obsolete. Computers, cell phones, email etc. have solved the communication problem, something we never dreamed would happen in our lifetime.

Footnote:

The small building to the left of my house is the garage that I built in the summer of 1987, which was described in a previous letter. Fr. Duffy helped me lay the concrete floor. I did the rest pretty much by myself. It was not a complicated building. Nevertheless, the students, teachers, and even the headmaster, were quite amazed that a priest could do building.

St. Paul the Apostle Center

August 6th, 1987

Dear Dorothy,

Received both your letters of July 15 and 17 on the same day, August 3. Thanks be to God they came a little faster than usual. Yesterday, August 5, I was in Shinyanga town and called Don. I got through right away with the new phone system put in by the Japanese. It is great to hear that Don is doing O.K. in his recovery. Thank you very much for writing right away.

I received a letter from Jack today giving a little more information. But he wrote before the operation. It is wonderful what they can do now. Both Floyd and Don have been given extra years which would not have been possible just a few years ago.

Today is a national holiday, the Muslim feast day Id El Had, and thus no school. I always like these days so I can catch up on a few things. I also want to put a few finishing touches on my garage. It really came out nice. The doors and windows are now in. My new car is in there now. I sleep better at night knowing that thieves can't break in. I still have my Volkswagen Combi sitting in the yard. The side mirror was stolen about 2 weeks ago. There is an African doctor, Emmanuel Mwandu, who works at Kolandoto hospital about 5 miles from here, who is buying it. He will pay me in Shillings. I have already told the Bishop I will donate this money to the youth center for helping to pay for the furniture, even before I knew that I was going to be assigned there. Now that I am going there it is even better. Also $150,000 has been received from Maryknoll to complete the buildings at the Youth Center. There are 6 buildings and the work there is only half finished. The plan is that the house and the library (part of which will be a small chapel) will be finished so that I can move in there, when I get back from leave next summer.

Enclosed is a check from Mrs. Grant for my account. I hear from her grandson, Dennis, now and then who is in the seminary. He joined the Legionaries of Christ, a rather strict organization. The Legionaries have a lot of strict rules and old fashion ways similar to when I was in the seminary on discipline etc. which I think is great.

I am happy you keep in touch with the McDaniels and let them know that we care. Greetings to Deb, Margaret and John and all.

Love and payers,

Fr. Marvin

My brother Don had a serious heart attack in August 1987. He was 52 years old and had seemed in excellent health. He had by-pass surgery and recovered. He had another heart attack 10 years later which incapacitated him. He also came down with MS. He lived until August 13, 2008. The last couple of years of his life were lived out in a nursing home. Floyd was my twin sister's husband.

Dr. Mwandu wanted to buy my Volkswagen Kombi. I gave it to him at a reduced price because he was African. I was surprised when he didn't want to sign the transfer of ownership in my presence. As it turned out, he was not buying it for himself but for some Arab friends in Shinyanga town who wanted to get the vehicle at a discount. (not many truly honest people around)

St. Paul the Apostle Center
Shinyanga Secondary School
Tanzania

Aug. 19, 1987

Dear Dorothy,

Today is Wednesday and with my new school schedule, I don't have any classes. I think it is the first time that I have had one day free from all classes. It really makes it nice if I want to do something or go someplace. One of our Fathers, Joe Reinhart who is the director of the language school, went home in April to have a by-pass operation. He had been having heart problems for some time and now seems as fit as ever. I hope our brother Don is progressing nicely and will be able to go back to work soon.

My trip to Musoma was much easier this time. Fr. Dick Hochwalt and I went together in my new pick-up. On the way we stopped at Bariadi where there was a big celebration going on for the blessing of a new church. Fr. Herb Gappa has been working on this church for 8 years. With all the shortages, building is a difficult task. Bishop Castor Sequa gave a nice talk after the blessing. He is trying to build a cathedral in Shinyanga next to the youth center where I am going and is experiencing some of the same difficulties.

When In Musoma, I tried out our new radio connection with Dar e Salaam which is a distance of 700 miles. The new radios work great. Almost as good as talking on the telephone except that you have to push a button when you are talking. This new system was approved by the government because it isn't powerful enough to reach worldwide but only locally. The plan is to put the radios in 16 different places. A man from the company in Dar es Salaam who is an expert is here to put them in. This is a real break- through especially when we think of the past many years with zero communication..

I am going ahead with some remote plans for the youth center. Fr. Ed Philips, our present procurator in Dar, is ordering the fridge, stove, and deep freeze from Holland. It will probably take about 8 months to get here and so by the time I am ready to go there, these things should be here.

I am delighted to hear that your daughter, Deb has a new job with such nice hours. She deserves a break and I am really happy for her.

Hope all goes well, much love,
Fr. Marv

St. Paul the Apostle Center

Sept. 23, 1987

Dear Dorothy,

Many thanks for your letter of August 26. Quite remarkable to hear that Don can go back to work half days. Sounds alike our cousins Joe and Edythe are in good health.

Traveling is not so easy and can be very tiring. But they have a very youthful spirit.

There is no school this week because of the mid-term break, and so I decided to take off for a few days to visit around the Musoma missions, something I should be doing as part of my responsibility as consulter to the regional superior. In fact I am writing this letter from the African sisters farm at Baraki where Fr. Art Willie is pastor and sort of a jack of all trades. The sisters have about 2000 acres which are part cattle ranch and part farm. Fr. Willie has built a huge damn, blocking an overflow of lake Victoria. He just finished it this year and it is wonderful for irrigating the crops behind the damn. He also put up a windmill on the shore of Lake Victoria which is almost 2 miles from here, which pumps clean water for all the household chores. There are 10 professed sisters here and about 30 postulants. It is quite an impressive operation and shows what can be done with a little knowledge and dedication.

I plan to visit two other missions and then go back to our regional headquarters at the language school in Musoma on Friday. Saturday morning I'll head back to Shinyanga taking with me 470 day-old chicks from Makoko Center which Andrew Veck, the German volunteer, asked for my help. My enclosed cabin in the back of my pickup is now finished and so I carry as many 6 passengers back there protected from the sun and dust. Also, when I carry luggage, it can be locked up. I came to Musoma with 3 of our students who

> *live up this way. Otherwise they would not have been able to go home for a short vacation.*
>
> *I hope Harold Scott is recovering from his operation. Please tell him I am remembering him in my prayers.*
> *Till next time, much love,*
> *Fr. Marv*

Footnote:

Fr. Art Willie was very impressive. He was one of the first Maryknollers to come to Africa. For many years he was in charge of training catechists as the catechetical center in Musoma diocese. As noted above, the dam he built for the sisters was quite a feat in engineering. With the dam, the sisters were able to irrigate their rice crop (and other crops) all year around. There is no shortage of water in Lake Victoria. It is a matter of harnessing it.

My brother Don, was another very impressive man. He started out as a surveyor in Minneapolis and later was asked to be the supervisor for Hennepin County's deeds. He had 20 people under him and was very well liked.

St. Paul the Apostles Center

Oct. 3, 1987

Dear Dorothy,

Many thanks for your letter of Sept, 9 which arrived a couple of days ago. I am happy to hear you enjoyed your retreat at the Franciscan retreat center at Prior Lake.

Retreats bring us many blessings and most of all help us to see what is really important in life.

My last letter was written at Baraki in Musoma diocese. I enjoyed my trip up there very much. Also, I got a chance to visit with Sr. Janet Srebalus, the Maryknoll sister I had worked with for 5 years in Dar es Salaam and whom I have not seen in about 9 years. She is now back in Tanzania after finishing her work in the U.S. and is not stationed in Musoma Diocese.

A couple of days ago I went to Ndoleleji Mission, which is Fr. Jim Travis's parish about 45 miles from here. I wanted to offer Jim my condolences over the death of his dad. When I got there in the late afternoon, I discovered, Fr. Jim had not returned yet. There are now two American lay missionaries there, both nurses. I had a nice visit with them and also was invited to supper. About 10 P.M. when I was going back to Fr. Jim's house, Fr. Jim appeared. He had just returned and I had the opportunity to offer my condolences and get the details of his dad's death. I think that Fr. Jim is much relieved that his dad's suffering is over. He had been sick for a very long time.

Yesterday I had a big surprise when Fr.George Smith, the White Father I used to work with in Dar e salaam and a very good friend, showed up at my door. He had flown to Mwanza and by good luck got a lift in a land rover with a couple of Africans coming this way. Fr. George is now the vocation director for the White Fathers and since they welcome African lads into their society, Fr. George is moving around to give talks in various schools. There is one boy here in our school whom he has been corresponding with for some time. I am going to take Fr. George into Shinyanga town and want him to see the unfinished youth center that I have been assigned to finish. Keep well, Dorothy and God bless you.

Much love,

Fr. Marvin

St. Paul Center
Shinyanga Secondary School

Oct. 15, 1987

Dear Dorothy,

Many thanks for your letter of Sept. 18 which arrived a few days ago. Last week there were a couple of days without school because of special examinations, so I drove Fr. George Smith (whom I mentioned in my last letter) down to Tabora, 120 miles South of here, where he wanted to visit some youth interested in the White Fathers. I have been wanting to go down there anyways since there is a very good Catholic Bookstore and printing press there. I brought back about 10 cases of bibles and various books which I will use not only here but also in the future at my new assignment to the youth center in Shinyanga.

Today there is no school since the place is being made ready for graduation which is Saturday, the day after tomorrow. In the morning there will be an open- house and each department will have a display. Some of the boys, in fact, have just arrived to help set up our religious education display. We have quite a few books, maps and visual aids which should be of interest to the guests who come for the graduation.

I had three Irish SMA Fathers for supper and overnight 2 days ago. One is Fr. Dan Cashman, just back from leave, who will be taking my place here. The superior wanted to check the place out. I think he was quite impressed. It is really a nice place, well equipped, active, etc. Fr. Dan is quite happy to come here. We haven't set any definite date yet. We will wait for the Bishop's advice and additional work to be complete at the youth center. The way I see it, Dan will probably be coming here after Easter next year.

The boys are waiting for me so best I go and put them to work. I didn't get a card out to Deb for her birthday. Anyhow, a belated HAPPY BIRTHDAY DEB...Lots of love. I hope all goes well...

Love and prayers,
Fr Marvin

P.S. Since mail is so slow, a Happy Thanksgiving to all.
I was very surprised to hear that the Twins are in the World Series, and would be even more surprised if they win it.

St. Paul the Apostle Center

Oct. 31, 1987

Dear Dorothy,

Thanks much for your letter of Oct. 6. The letter with the pictures arrived 2 days later. I am still waiting for the package from Sr. Leonarda with the kit to help measure the ear of the deaf, blind boy, Juma. (Sr. Leonarda saw a specialist who agreed to help one of our boys to hear again). Thanks for the pictures. They turned out very nice. Most of these were ordered by the boys. But I will send out a few of the youth to benefactors at Christmas.

I was delighted to hear that the Twins won the World Series. The BBC (British broadcasting Company), gave the scores on the evening news, although they usually don't cover American baseball during the regular season's play.

We have had a couple of good rains since I last wrote, although now it is dry again. The rains were sufficient to bring out all the leaves on the trees and turn the grass green. Don't know if you are familiar with bougainvillea, a vine which grows in the tropics. Bougainvillea grows all year around since they are drought resistant, but right now they are especially full. I have them both in front of the house and in front of the church.

Schools are going along fine. The form IV's are finishing now and begin their final on Nov. 2, just one month left for the rest and we begin the longer vacation. I have started making some shelving for the new place in my spare time. During the vacation time, I will spend a lot more time making furniture etc.   God bless you.

Love,

Fr. Marv

St. Paul the Apostle Center

Nov. 23, 1987

Dear Dorothy,

Thanks very much for your letter of Nov.1 which arrived a couple of days ago. Sounds like the people really had a bash over the victory by the Twins. There haven't been too many victories in Minnesota. Really gave the people a glow to be on top for a change. ...You are getting ready for winter. Your new door will make this winter easier.

Here, classes are now finished for the year. Exams are going on this week.   I gave one this morning to the Form 5's. The students leave at the end of the week for vacation. On Thursday, Thanksgiving, the Maryknollers in the area. Will be getting together in Shinyanga town at Dr. Kerry Watrin's place. Kerry and his nurse-wife, Terry, are Maryknoll lay missionaries, both in their early thirties. I will make a couple of mango pies for the celebration.

Since I last wrote, I have been up to Musoma for a regional council meeting. This was a quicky. On Friday, Nov. 13 , I drove 90 miles to Mwanza, picked up Fr. John Eyble, our assistant regional superior, and continued to Musoma. At one stretch we cross what is called the corridor, where a narrow section of the Serengeti plains extends out to Lake Victoria. There is an old narrow bridge made of steel beams across a narrow river which was not replaced when the new tarmac road was put in. It seems like some hooligans took the bolts out and the bridge collapsed. The construction company has made a detour about a quarter of a mile downstream, and put in a Bailey Bridge (used for temporary bridges during the war). We had no trouble getting across both going and coming because the river hadn't risen yet when we came back on Monday, we ran into heavy rains, but we got across before everything was wiped out.

 Hope you had a wonderful Thanksgiving. I've got to get busy this week in sending out some Christmas cards.
Love,
Fr. Marvin

P.S. The ear kit from Sr. Leonarda arrived. We have taken the impression of the young lad's ear and sent it back to Sister.

St. Paul the Apostle Center
Shinyanga Secondary School

Jan. 6, 1988

Dear Dorothy,
        Thanks much for your letter of Dec. 1. I got back from Nairobi on Dec. 23 and your letter was brought over by Mr.

Gedi, the clerk at the school who takes care of the mail...Christmas was very nice here. The children of the teachers helped me decorate the church. Since I made a stable last year, it was easy to get things ready. We had mass at 8 P.M. on Christmas Eve and again on Christmas day at 9 A.M. The chapel was not entirely full since the students are not here, but there was a good crowd of villagers whose young people led the singing for the community here of teachers, staff members and their families.

The Sunday after Christmas I had a wedding scheduled here at the regular Sunday mass at 9 A.M. The young bride from the village of Utemini, Modesta, was here with her attendants at 7 A.M. She had her beautiful white wedding gown in her satchel and I gave her the library to get herself ready. The boy, Boniface, is from Wila, about 18 miles from here. They were both in the day before to go over the wedding ceremony and go to confession. The boy said he would be coming with a big truck to carry his relatives and friends. 9:30 rolled around and Boniface still had not shown up. To pass the time I began writing up the marriage document which is sent to the government, and put the data in my own marriage register. About a quarter to 10 a young man came pounding at my door all sweaty and out of breath. He reported there had been a terrible accident. The truck with the wedding party had turned over about a mile from here. I got my pickup out of my garage and rushed down there with the lad in the front seat, who brought the report.

It was really a mess. The truck was laying on its side. About half the people were badly injured. Some had broken legs. Others had gashes in their heads. Many were bruised and bleeding. Most of the injured were men since they were on the outer side of the truck bed. The women who were in the middle were somewhat protected. I loaded up my pickup with about 10 people who could walk and rushed off to the diamond mine's hospital where I got help from several nurses and the police. The police came in two Land rovers and the nurses came with me. It took several trips back and forth to get all the injured to the hospital. (only about a mile and a half
away) . We took the ones with the broken bones first, and when it was all finished, filled up two wards in the hospital with a total of about 30 people.

The bridegroom and the best man were with the driver in the cab and were not hurt. It was after 12 noon when I finally got back to the chapel to report that the wedding was cancelled. I said mass, however, for the filled church. Modesta's father was very disappointed since he had spent a lot of money for food, had killed a big cow, etc. for the celebration. I would have preferred to go on with the wedding, but the bridegroom said no, so that was that.

Yesterday I went over to the hospital to check on the progress of the injured. Only those with broken bones and concussions were still there (about 10). The others had been discharged a few days earlier.

The work on the new youth center in Shinyanga town is progressing. The house for the chaplain is now finished. Brother Cyril with his workers did the work. It was quite a job because he decided to raise the roof one foot. He thought the ceilings on the original plan were too low. The fridge, stove, deep freeze and washing machine which I had ordered from Holland, arrived in Shinyanga and are being stored with Brother Cyril until I go to the center. I am making a few pieces of the furniture myself. I have finished the kitchen counter with cabinets below and am transporting it to the center today in the back of my pickup.

Next week we have our regional meeting at the language school in Musoma. On the 18th of January, school begins again. The vacation time is fleeting by......I received a nice letter from Margaret. Good to hear things are going well. A happy New Year to all of you... Till next time.

Love and prayers,
Fr. Marvin

Footnote:

After a little investigation, it was discovered that the young man who was driving the borrowed truck did not have a license. He was not an experienced driver. He was going much too fast when he miscalculated the small bridge he was crossing. It was very fortunate that nobody was killed. The wedding finally took place about a year later.

Nairobi

Feb. 2, 1988
Feast of the Presentation

Dear Dorothy,

I have written to Sr. Leonarda and want to write to you too, to tell you the latest and to explain why I am in Nairobi. After the regional assembly in mid-January, I was experiencing some dizziness and chest discomfort. Our lay missionary doctor in Shinyanga, knowing the history of coronary problems in my family, suggested that I be flown to Nairobi by the "Flying Doctor" service for tests and examinations. The small plane flew in to the Mwadui Diamond mine's airport (just 10 minutes away from my house at the secondary school) on January 25 at 9:45 A.M. When we arrived in Nairobi an hour and a half later, I was taken immediately by ambulance to Nairobi hospital. I was given a room and the heart specialist, Doctor Silverstein, who is an American, set me up for a cardiogram, blood pressure etc. The next day he put me on the treadmill for a stress test. I passed all these tests with flying colors and he assured me that I do not have a heart problem. The next several days I was given all kinds of tests - blood - sugar, etc etc, the results of which I will get this Thursday, Feb. 4th.

I am now at the Maryknoll house taking it easy and getting some exercise (tennis) in the afternoon and feeling fine. I don't think there is anything wrong with me and that a little R and R will not cure. I guess I have been pushing a little too hard the past couple of years. The regional superior wants me up here for 2 weeks' vacation which is O.K. by me. I will let you know how all the tests come out.

> *Greetings to all... Love and prayers....*
> *Fr. Marvin*

Footnote:

We had two lay missionary doctors from the U.S. working in Shinyanga diocese. Dr. Kerry Watrin was in Shinyanga town with his wife, Terry, a nurse; Dr. Tom Tem was at Ndoleleji Parish out in the boondocks. They received very little salary and were very dedicated.

The assistant doctor to Dr. Silverstein (an Indian from India) asked me some questions about my work load and schedule. He said, "I have a brother just like you. He thinks he can solve all the problems in the world." The doctor suggested that I cut my schedule in half and this would solve my health problems.

Footnote:

My sister Dorothy's husband, Wally, died on Feb. 7, 1961 at age 43. Every year I said mass for him on that day.

Nairobi

Feb. 7th, 1988

Dear Dorothy,

I now have all the results of my medical examination. I do not have a heart problem. In fact, I did very well in the treadmill test considering my age. Everything else is normal too. I even got a chance to see a very good dentist, Dr.

Paschareia, an Indian who put a crown on my broken tooth. So I am in good shape all around and hope to head back to Tanzania in 4 or 5 days if I can pick up a ride from someone going down.

This morning I offered mass for Wally and have had a relaxing day. Later on this afternoon, three of the other fathers and I will play a little tennis on the clay courts at Loretto girls' school, a short distance from here. The courts are open to outsiders on Sunday.

Hi to Deb and Margaret. Am writing to Marlys, Don and Jack too.

Love and Prayers,
Fr. Marvin

Footnote:
Deb and Margaret were adopted daughters of Dorothy. Jack and Don were my siblings. .

St. Paul the Apostle Center

Mach 19, 1988
Dear Dorothy,
Seems like your birthday has a way of sneaking up on me, and I always forget to send a letter early enough to arrive before your birthday. Anyhow, A VERY HAPPY BIRTHDAY. I have marked in my mass calendar to say mass for you on the 28 of March which is the day after Palm Sunday.

Thanks for your letter of Feb. 28. Sorry to hear that you had strep throat. That can be mighty uncomfortable. A couple of weeks ago I came down suddenly with malaria with chills and a temperature of 102. I took a dose of chloroquine diphosphate which proved to be ineffective since the parasites seemed to have built up a resistance to it. So I tried a strong dose of fansidar, the drug I took when I had malaria so bad a couple of years ago. That was 6 PM in the evening and by the next morning my temp was back to normal. I couldn't teach for a couple of days and just rested. I am in tip- top shape right now. Perhaps I had some malaria bugs in me last January when I was having all that trouble. After taking fansidar I feel better now than I have in a long time.

Tomorrow the Catholic boys will have a celebration to say farewell to the form 6 boys who will graduate in a couple of weeks. They have been working hard this week preparing songs, to which they sing , make dance routines , called "jiving" like the ones you saw on the video I had made. This year they have made up an English song to which they dance to which goes like this: "Take your time when you are feeling gloomy; take your time, you gona feel all right. Jesus Christ, the Son of God, he came to see, to save and set me free." I would say that is a pretty good philosophy to live by.

Have a wonderful celebration on your birthday...
My love and prayers.
Fr. Marvin

St. Paul the Apostle Center

April 8, 1988

Dear Dorothy,

Thanks very much for your letter of March 13 with Easter Greetings. I had a very nice Easter. I had 52 youth here for a retreat during Holy week which was delightful. This week there is no school since it is the mid-term break. And there are sporting events going on at the schools for about 900 students from all over the region. Most carry sponge mattresses which they just lay on the floor. Today is the last day of the events..

I am spending some time this week packing up my things. I still have a lot of supplies left. I will give some to Fr. Dan Cashman who is taking my pace. He has already brought some of his own supplies which he left off here the other day. I will store all my things in one of the containers and won't move anything until I return from home leave.

I think that in one of your letters you asked about the new house where I will move into at the youth center. It is not quite as big as this one. I would say it is about the size of yours without the basement. The kitchen is very small. I have to do a lot with cabinets to make room for everything. The small deep fridge and fridge will be out in the dining area. There is an extension on the roof in the front which can be completed below which will make a nice porch. I plan to screen that in so that there will be a mosquito free place to sit and also to receive guests.

I am enclosing a check I received from Monsignor Flemming of St. Olaf's parish in downtown Minneapolis. Please put it into my account.

Fr. Dan Cashman is moving in here on April 18th. Which will give me some freedom to do things I have to finish before leaving. Also I have another meeting in Musoma on April 18. Till next time - my greetings to all.

Love,
Fr. Marvin

St. Paul Center
Shinyanga Secondary School

April 30, 1988

Dear Dorothy,

Thanks much for your letter of Palm Sunday which just arrived yesterday. That one took over a month. Good to hear that all is going along O.K. You have it sized up pretty well regarding the many things to be done here before I leave. Fr. Dan Cashman, the Irish SMA Father, is now here. He arrived about 2 weeks ago and was present during the time I had to go to Musoma for the board meeting. I was gone about a week and a half because after the meeting I had some visitations to do in our missions in North Mara. These were interviews to help each individual Maryknoller in their planning process. We are all supposed to have a plan even if it is just mental and talking it over with someone helps to make one

209

think in these terms rather than just going on from day to day without any plan at all.

Things went well during my safari except that it was slow going because there has been so much rain. Many of the roads were muddy and slippery, but I got stuck only once and it just so happened that there was a big truck behind me filled with about 15 men who pushed me out.

Fr Dan Cashman is a very good man. He was headmaster himself in a high school in Nigeria for 10 years, so he really understands the school apostolate. Perhaps I mentioned in my last letter that I am helping with the retreat at Wila from May 16-20. Wila is 15 miles from here. Fr. Tom Shea, who lives there and usually takes care of all the arrangements, has been in the U.S. since last November when his mother had a stroke. She has been in a coma ever since and Tom has no brothers or sisters to help.

After that I will be going to Nairobi to get my plane for Rome. From there, I will fly to Yugoslavia and spend 5 days at Medjugorje where I will make my own retreat since it will not be possible to make it at Wila with all the work I have to do supervising the cooking and taking care of all the physical arrangements. Brother John Wohead wants to go with me to Rome and Yugoslavia. I hope this works out because it will be much more interesting to be with someone when traveling. Brother John also has a great devotion to Our Lady, which will make it a real sharing experience.

I expect to land in Minneapolis the evening of June 7. I will drop a note to Marlys and Floyd with the flight number in case they are able to pick me up. I am going to Wila right now to check out the place for the retreat. There are some good workers there which will make the job much easier.

Greetings to all....

Love and prayers,

Fr. Marvin

Chapter III

Trip to Medjugorje to Prepare for New Job to Finish New Youth Center in Shinyanga Tow

I remember the date when I was at Medjugorje in Yugoslavia because I was there for the feast of Corpus Christi, 1988. We were about 20 priests concelebrating mass at St. James' Church on this great feast day. A bearded priest came up to me during the "kiss of peace" greetings and said, "Marvin Deutsch, peace be with you." I was surprised that someone would recognize me in Yugoslavia. After a few words, I recognized his voice. It was Mayknoller, Fr. Ed, "Tex" Schollman. I had not seen him since he left Tanzania about 10 years earlier. He was on a leave of absence from Maryknoll, was studying for a degree in counseling in Texas, and had joined a group of pilgrims from there and had come to Medjugorje. It was a pleasant surprise to see him. I spent most of the day with him. Medjugorje turned out to be a wonderful and fascinating experience. It is worthwhile to start from the beginning.

It was about 7 P.M. in the evening. Brother John Wohead and I were at the Rome airport waiting for a Yugoslavian plane to fly to Belgrade. The plane was late, but this was not unusual. We had been informed by others that the Yugoslav airline rarely was on time. They said it was one of the quirks of Communism. A young lady, overhearing our conversation about visiting the holy shrine of Medjugorje, asked if she could join us. She said she was coming from Chicago and on vacation. She had an American friend who was working as a house servant in one of the many hostels that had sprung up to accommodate the pilgrims, and was on her way to see her. We said - no problem, you are welcome to join us.

The plane finally arrived from Belgrade and prepared for its return flight. We all boarded and were on our way. My big concern was that we would be a couple of hours late getting into Belgrade and therefore lose our connective flight from Belgrade to Mostar, the city only 18 miles from Medjugorje. Well, when we arrived in Belgrade, we were happy to find out that we did not miss our flight after all. That flight was also delayed and so perhaps the saying about things don't run on time under communism was to our advantage at this point. Actually the fight to Mostar was very late in leaving. We didn't get into Mostar, only about an hour and a half away, until 2 A.M. in the morning. Judy, the young lady with us, was quite upset. Her baggage had been lost and all she had with her was her purse. As we were discussing what we should do since it was in the middle of the night, a man approached and asked us if we wanted a taxi to go to Medjugorje. He said he could take us there for $15.00 ($5.00 each). It didn't take us long to decide. Yes, we will be delighted to take your cab. Judy would have to deal with her baggage problem later.

And so up the mountain we climbed, congratulating ourselves on finding a solution of how to get to Medjugorje. As we neared the top of the mountain, perhaps about 20 minutes later, the cab driver suddenly pulled off the road. He said to us in a gruff voice, "Get out". Oh, oh, this is it. This guy is probably not a cab driver at all, but a criminal, and will probably shake us down for all we are worth. When we got out of the cab, much to our relief, the cab driver pointed down to the city below, and said, "Nice view". We could see the lights from the town, standing out clearly, which indeed was quite a sight to see. However, it was chilly outside, and we were very tired. It was very comforting to get back into the cab and be on our merry way, knowing this guy was an o.k. guy who would not rip us off, but would take us to our destination.

When we arrived at Medjugorje, it was 3 A.M. in the morning. There was not a soul in sight - no cars - nothing. The streets dimly light by the adjacent lamps, reminded us that everyone except perhaps for us, was sound asleep and not a bit interested in the lonely car looking for its destination.

Judy told the cab driver to look for the Jozo restaurant. She said that her girlfriend lived right next to the store. The cab driver went up and down the streets, looking, looking. Actually he turned out to be a pretty nice guy who was not trying to add on the amount we agreed on. Finally in desperation, I saw a residence with the front light on. It looked like people might still be up. So I said, "let me go and knock on the door and perhaps we can find out where the Jozo restaurant is." Judy went with me. I knocked on the door. In a minute or two, it opened and lo and behold, Judy's friend appeared. It was like a miracle, or at least like finding a needle in a haystack. After Judy and her girlfriend hugged each other, I asked the girl what she might be doing up so late. She said that there was a group of pilgrims there from Milwaukee. One of the lady's wanted to stay up and talk. After the lady finally went to bed, I had to finish my work, doing the laundry etc. And that is why I am still up…. We thanked the cab driver and gave him a generous tip. Judy's friend said the place was completely filled up. Judy could stay with her in her room, but Brother John and I, although without a room, could sleep on the floor in the living room.

Thank God it was almost dawn. I found it very hard to sleep on the marble floor, although Brother John seemed to be out like a light. When I heard the bell ringing for morning mass, I got up and stiffly walked out the front door and headed for St. James' Church about a half mile away. I got there just in time for the German mass. (Every hour, a different tour group had their own mass in their own language.) After Mass I returned to find everybody at the hostel having breakfast. They invited me to join them. I met one fellow, Robert, from Milwaukee, who befriended me. We were to meet off and on the next few days.

After breakfast, Brother John and I went to the parish office. The priest there, Fr. Baltazar spoke English well and helped many people find a place to stay with the parishioners during their time at Medjugorje. Brother John told Fr. Baltazar that we wanted to be in the room in the rectory when Our Blessed Mother appears to the young visionaries. Fr. Baltazar said that Mary no longer appears in the rectory but up in the choir loft of the church and no one has permission to be there. He said the Bishop, (Bishop Zanic) had forbidden it. Shortly after, a small boy of about 4 appeared at the door. Fr. Baltazar said that we should just follow him and we will be led to the place of our residence. Sure enough, he took us through some grapevine fields to his home where his mother and father were building a large addition on to their house to accommodate pilgrims. These additions were springing up all over the place with the ever increasing number of pilgrims. It worked well for both sides since this small town originally did not have hotels.

Brother John and I sort of went our separate ways during the next few days. I ran into my new friend, Robert, now and then. On one occasion we were sitting outside on the ground on the western side of the church. The rosary was being said with the leader inside the church speaking in Croatian, and everybody else answering in their own language, either in the church or in groups outside the church. There were so many people that it was impossible for all to be in the church. Suddenly Robert said to me, "Look at the sun, it is dancing in the sky!" Sure enough, I could look right at the late afternoon sun without harm to my eyes. It looked like a large host and was pulsating. This lasted for about 10 minutes. Robert caught it all in his video camera. (He later sent me a copy of the video which I showed to many people as time went on.)

Before I get too far into my story, I want to explain my reason for wanting to go to Medjugorje. As you have read previously, Bishop Castor Sekwa had asked me to finish the work at the youth Center in Shinyanga town. When I saw the 4 partially finished buildings which had been sitting there for 5 years without any progress, it seemed to me that the Bishop was asking me to do what I considered, "Mission Impossible". Weeds had grown up everywhere, making it even look more desolate. For example, a tree had grown up in the auditorium, now perhaps 8 feet tall. It was almost impossible to buy any building supplies in Tanzania since the country was bankrupt because of the ongoing war with Idi Amin of Uganda.. I would need electrical and plumbing materials. Even things like two-by-fours were now difficult to buy in our area. Anyhow, I had agreed to take the project on. Brother Cyril had agreed to finish the priest's residence so that I could have a place, at least, to live. Brother Cyril was negotiating with the Indian contractor, Mr. Patel, to see if he would agree to finish the project with the new grant from Maryknoll, $150,000. He wanted much, much more. His final assessment was 225,000 dollars. I said to Brother Cyril that I would be willing to do the contracting myself, get my own supplies from overseas and find my own workers.

That was the reason I went to Medjugorje - to get the help of Our Blessed Mother. I said to her (in my heart) "This project is much too big for me, but it is not too big for you. I will go to Medjugorje and pray. I will go to the U.S. and buy the needed materials and have them shipped over in a couple of containers. I will ask the Bishop if we can change the name of the center, calling it "Queen of Peace Youth Center" rather than "Charles Luwanda" Youth Center (the original name picked out by Fr. Tokus at least 5 years earlier). Before I joined the seminary in 1949, I had consecrated my life to the Blessed Virgin Mary (St. Louis Demontfort Consecration). This project was just another step along the way of consecration.

St. James' Church at Medjugorje

The cross marks the spot where Mary first appeared to the young people at Medjugorje, June 24, 1981.They were up on the hill behind the place where they lived taking care of their sheep and goats.

The town of Medjugorje can be seen a long way off in the background.

Just beyond the cross, is the present day statue of Mary. This statue is the object or end point of the climb on "Apparition Hill." Apparition Hill is perhaps a mile from St. James' Church. This is usually the first long walk taken by pilgrims. They often say the rosary on the way.

221

The second long walk is about a half mile from the church in a different direction. The walk is up a very steep and jagged mountain called "Cross Mountain". The parishioners built a cross (top picture) on the top in 1933 commemorating the 1900 anniversary of the crucifixion of Jesus. Little did they know that about 50 years later, this cross would be the object for many from all over the world to come and climb up it's steep and rocky path to pray at the Stations of the Cross, and honor Jesus our redeemer and Savior.

This picture is the view of the town from the height of the cross.

A man I met at Medjugorje. I met so many people from all over the world. Everyone was so friendly.

One of the visionaries, Vicka (holding the beam). She gave a formal talk every day outside of her house. Vicka was the most outgoing of the visionaries.

A popular painting of Our Lady, Queen of Peace of
Medjugorje.

What impressed me most at Medjugorje? What I
think was the most significant was the great number of
people going to confession. The confessions, for the most
part, were heard outside, in the empty space on the eastern
side of the church. Sometimes there were as many as 15
priests hearing confessions, each one in his own language.
All one did was pick up a sign with your language on it, sit
down on a folding chair out in the open, and welcome the
people. It seemed like everyone had a tremendous desire

225

to confess. Even Protestants would ask. They could be heard, of course, but could not receive absolution, but a blessing instead. The reason why I consider this so significant is because after the Vat. Council, the use of the Sacrament of Confession almost disappeared. I have always considered this as an aberration. Mary was getting people back to confession again, a sacrament that would change the lives of many and lead them in God's grace along the road leading to Salvation. The word, "conversion" sums up the whole meaning of Medjugorje.

There were many other experiences that could be written about Medjugorje, but I think it suffices to say that my going there was a very important step in my missionary career at this time of my life, especially in getting Mary's help in the work that lay ahead in building and opening the youth center. When I arrived at my sister house back home in Minneapolis, I had much to do in ordering and buying the many materials and supplies that I would need. For one thing, I did not have a copy of the plans of the youth center. They had been sent to Dar es Salaam for simplification. There was a German architect headquartered there who worked with the Episcopal conference. He was asked to modify and simplify the plans. However, unfortunately he was killed in an auto accident. He was traveling at night along the Morogoro road and did not see a truck which had broken down and parked alongside of the road. The German was killed instantly. No one knew where he had put the plans for the youth center.

After I was in Minneapolis a few days I went to work. I was walking down Lake Street and 27th avenue and saw a business sign, "Electrical Contractor". I went in and asked the receptionist if the contractor was in. She asked who I was and she would inform her boss. A few minutes later, he called me in. I explained to him that I was a missionary working in Tanzania, Africa and need some assistance in knowing what electrical materials to buy for shipment overseas. He asked for the plans of the buildings. When I said I didn't have any, that the plans were lost but I could give him a description of the buildings, he got very angry and told me "to get the hell out of his office". When I walked by the secretary, she looked the other way. I guess she felt sorry for me that her boss had treated me so rudely.

About a week later, I decided to go up to Hill City to visit my good friend and grade school classmate, Ed Wortman. Ed was a builder and kind of jack of all trades. I was sure that he wouldn't throw me out because I didn't have the plans. Also, I needed a little encouragement. This whole project seemed to be getting more difficult by the day. Hill City was a couple of hours drive north of Minneapolis. There was a ski resort there called Quadna that Ed and a friend of his had built and opened up. They had received a grant from the government for this project to help improve the economy in this so called depressed area. Ed and his partner had sold out, but Ed decided to stay in the area. He was now doing some building for another contractor and also selling real estate.

Ed and his wife, Marie, were dear old friends, and were very happy to see me.   In the evening we played "Uno", a fun game that makes all feel very light hearted. When I explained to Ed the purpose of my visit, he was very sympathetic and said he knew of a guy, Bill Hess, who was a master builder and remodeler. Bill was a very decent fellow and certainly would be of help.   Ed called Bill and made an appointment for me to see him after he got home from work. Bill had just purchased a former grade school from the County which he was going to turn into a residence for himself and his wife and also sort of a center for his operations. Bill showed us around and tried to answer my questions about electrical purchases I would need for the youth center project.   He decided he didn't know enough about electricity and suggested we call his friend, Dennis Kluge, an electrical contractor who lived in Rapid City about 25 miles away.   Ed called Dennis and Dennis said he could see us the following day.   I felt good about that and thought that things were getting on track and it seemed like our Blessed Mother was taking over.

The following day we went to see Dennis. He invited us into his home and introduced his wife, "Gabby." (I think she got this name because she was never found to be speechless) Dennis asked me to sketch everything I knew about the size of the buildings and asked about the voltage used, etc. He made a whole list of everything that would be needed and said he would order all these things for me from Viking Electric charging them to his account so that I would receive a contractor's discount.   After we were all finished and just as I was walking out the door, I turned to Dennis to thank him for his help. Off handedly I said, "You know Dennis, I don't know much about electricity. Why don't you come to Tanzania and supervise the job for me. I will pay your way over and back." Dennis looked at me seriously and said, "I have always wanted to go to Africa, what do you think, Gabby, should I go over and help the Father?" Gabby said, "I think you should do it, Honey." So I said, "Dennis, why don't you think it over. I'll call you in a couple of days to get your answer."

A day or two later, I returned to my sister, Dorothy's place, and a couple of days later called Dennis. He said, "I can do it, but it will have to be in January during the off season in Minnesota." I said, "That's just fine, Dennis. January will be better for me anyway since I have to send everything over in a container and by that time the containers will certainly have arrived. A few hours later, I got a call from Ed Wortman in Hill City. He said, " Bill Hess wants to know why you didn't invite him as well. He wants to go over there too.   All he asks in return is that you take them out hunting in the Serengeti Plains." I was really pleased about that call. Now I had an electrical contractor and a first class carpenter…. A few days later, my sister and I invited an old friend, Fran Lamosse over for supper. I was telling her about Dennis and Bill coming to Africa. As Fran was leaving, I said, "Hey Fran, why don't you come along too." She excitedly said, "I would like to do that. I can be chief cook and bottle washer." Actually, I had no intention of inviting Fran.   She was 65 years old and would be vulnerable to tropical diseases like malaria. I didn't want that responsibility. But once Fran got something in her head, there was no one in this wide world that could stop her. She called me a few days later and said, "I am coming and I will pay my own way."

The rest of the summer went by quickly. I bought tons of building materials, some of them right at the location in New Holstein, Wisconsin, where the Salvatorians, Brother Regis and his crew packed and sent out the containers. A friend of mine, John Sharpe, talked to his son who had a big pick-up. We drove that to New Holstein with electrical supplies and many other things. It was a successful summer. I was filled with hope that this was no longer "Mission Impossible". Our Blessed Mother had taken over. Shortly after mid-August I left for Africa, flying by way of Europe. I arrived in Nairobi, Kenya from where my next letter will begin.

Nairobi

August 23, 1988

Dear Dorothy,

I am getting ready to leave Nairobi. I plan to go tomorrow after lunch and go as far as Kiricho where I will spend the night. There are some good hotels there. Brother Dave McKena and Sr. Maureen Myer are looking for a ride to Musoma and so I will have some company half way.

Since I left Minneapolis, a lot of things have happened. It was a wonderful experience to be at Cheshire, Connecticut and also spend some time with Mrs. Grant and the McCormack's. The flights to Rome and Nairobi were both very nice. The plane landed in Nairobi at 11 P.M. Friday, August 19th. There was a taxi driver there with a big sign with my name on it and so I got a free ride to the Maryknoll house from Archers, the travel agent who had arranged my itinerary.

Yesterday, Monday, I found the Interfreight office in town and gave all the papers to Mr. Hans Blasberg, the Kenya International general manager. There doesn't seem to be any problem except that Joan Baron's papers should have had a detailed list with value listed for each item. Hans said it will cost more without it.

I sent a package with some African cloth to Joan Baron, airmail today. The total cost was $90.00. I wrote to Joan asking that she send a check for this amount to you for my account.

I would like to spend a couple of more days here, but it is time to get going. My pickup was here when I arrived. The paint I had ordered was here also with all the export papers made out. I had the oil changed and a grease job done and so am ready to go. I have to get down to Shinyanga before Brother Cyril leaves and then back up to Musoma for the board meeting on August 30th, which means I will be doing a lot of driving.

Thanks again for your hospitality. It was a good time there and we did a lot of things. Hi to Deb.

Love and prayers,

Fr. Marvin

Footnote:

The reason for the visit to Hans Blasberg of Kenya International in Nairobi was to arrange for the transport of my two containers when they arrived from the U.S. The port of entry was Mombassa on the Kenyan coast. (The headquarters for the company was Düsseldorf, Germany). They would bring the containers by truck from Mombasa, Kenya all the way to Shinyanga, Tanzania, a distance of 900 miles. The border crossing between Kenya and Tanzania was the usual holdup. So many papers had to be filled out for customs etc. which usually took several days.

Queen of Peace Youth Center
P.O Box 47, Shinyanga, Tanzania

Sept. 8, 1988

Dear Dorothy,

On this, our Lady's birthday, I want to write a few lines. I am writing this from the youth center. I have been working here since Monday, Sept. 4. Seems like there is some visible progress already. I hired a painter who is making good progress on the classroom block. I am painting the cement on the outside a light orange trimmed with brown. The front part of the building can be painted completely since the cement is smooth. The back part and the sides are stucco but with a smooth section on the top and the bottom, and on the sides. This smooth part we are painting, but the stucco is just too difficult and would take too much paint, so we are leaving it the natural grey color. I have the priest's house all cleaned out. In fact, I am writing this from the little kitchen where I have set up a small folding table. Since the electricity is not yet connected, I have set up a single burner, bottle gas stove which works just fine for boiling water or whatever. I have been down to Tanesco, the electric company, several times trying to get them to come out and connect the electricity in the house temporarily until the entire electric system is put in, but so far no luck. I think the guy is looking for a bribe which I suppose I will have to pay if we want electricity....

Believe it or not, the man from the electric company came just now. I just talked to him. He said they can start working on the line tomorrow. I told him if he can do it quickly, I will buy him a case of beer. It's worth it so I can begin setting up the house and start making tables, cabinets, etc. Today, our Lady's birthday – she must have had something to do with this guy stopping by.

I have been to Musoma for the board meeting. I had just gotten back from Nairobi, having had a couple of days with Brother Cyril and then off again. The contractor, Mr. Patel, has left for England where he will spend about 4 *months. I am so glad we are off the hook with him. I can do it myself for half the price.*

I am staying at Buhangija (the Bishop's residence) at the present, using Brother Cyril's room. Brother Cyril has left for the U.S. to have his cataract surgery and vacation time. If we can gain good progress, and get the electricity, I plan to move in here in about 2 weeks' time. It is just about 3 PM now, and time for my workers to quit. I want to get a quick line off to Ed Wortman. I hope all goes well and you are having a beautiful fall

Greetings to all....

Love and prayers.....

Fr. Marvin

Footnote:

The Indian contractor, Mr. Patel, was reluctant to give up the temporary agreement he had made with Brother Cyril to finish the work on the 4 buildings of the youth center. He had hoped to make an enormous profit. He was holding out for $225,000. The grant we had from Maryknoll was $150,000. Since I was the person who offered to finish the project within budget, Mr. Patel became very angry with me. Before he left for England, he confronted me and said, "Before you came here I was getting along very well with Brother Cyril and the diocese. You have spoiled it all for me." Since I had ordered most of the building materials from the US. Which would arrive by container, I knew I could do it within budget. As we come to future letters when the youth center is completed, you will see that not only did I finish the project within budget, but added, two more buildings (hostels), a huge water tank, a cement tennis court, cement basketball court, a garage, and outdoor toilet, all within budget, and I still had $50,000 left over. This gives you some idea how much profit these contractors make. Mr. Patel said to me, "You can't build this place without me." Meaning I didn't have the expertise. I assured Mr. Patel, "I can build this place." What he didn't realize was that I had the Blessed Mother on my side and also I had two experts coming from Minnesota to help me.

Queen of Peace Youth Center
P.O. Box 47, Shinyanga, Tanzania

Dear Dorothy,

I got your letter of Sept. 7 stating that Aunt Catherine had suffered a stroke on the same day that Alice Saleck called saying that Aunt Catherine had died. I am happy that her suffering is now over and that she is with the Lord. I said mass for her the very next day. I am sure she is singing and rejoicing with the angels in heaven.

I have some real good news regarding the youth center. Yesterday morning (Sunday) the workers connected up the electricity in my house. They usually don't work on Sunday, but they did this special job which seems to indicate that there is somebody up there looking after things. I already have my electric stove and fridge connected and working. I plan to move in by Oct. 1.

Bishop John Kinney from Bismarck, N.D. is visiting here with two of his priests. They are checking out the possibility of sending a team here (priests and lay people) to work in Tanzania. I knew Bishop Kinney when he was a young priest stationed at St. Thomas parish in S.W. Minneapolis during the time I was on promotion. It's really nice to visit with these men. We had a concelebrated mass this morning with a mixture of English and Kiswahili.

I will ask one of these priests to mail this in the U.S. so that it won't take so long.

I am happy to hear all is going well and that you are having nice fall weather.

With love and prayers,
Fr. Marvin

Footnote:

There was a very good reason for the motivation to connect up the electricity even though it was Sunday when the workers for the electric company were off. I promised them a case of beer which certainly had a lot to do with it.

Bishop Kinney ended up choosing Northern Kenya as their choice of where to send their team. It was not too far from the Somali border which was a dangerous place to be. They were there a couple of years but eventually had to leave because of banditry of the Somalis who came across the border. They moved to Kericho diocese which was not a dangerous area to work.

Queen of Peace Youth Center
P.O. Box 47, Shinyanga
Tanzania

Oct. 22, 1988

Dear Dorothy,

Thank you for your letter of Sept. 30 with Sr. Leonarda's enclosed. It was nice that she could be with you for a few days and also share some of my letters since I have not had much time to write.

I am writing this letter from our regional headquarters in Musoma. I will return to Shinyanga tomorrow. I brought Fr. John Gorski who just finished a 3 day seminar on "The Urgency of Evangelization" up here from Shinyanga. John, who is a good friend of mine from our days together in Rome, is giving the same seminar in various places. He finished Musoma and Shinyanga. Fr. Hayes, our Regional Superior, will take him to Nairobi where John will also give a seminar. John stayed at my new place while in Shinyanga and was the very first guest to stay there. The electricity and water were on only about half the time, but we made out O.K.

We are making steady progress at the youth center. Most of the painting is done now in the library complex and in the classroom block. There is still much to do in the auditorium. I contracted out the making of the window frames and hope our diocesan workers can begin to finish the cement floor. The rough 4 inch concrete floor is in. There remains the 1 inch finish which is of fine cement.

Our electric and water supply should become steady as soon as the new 60 ton transformer is connected at the power station which will put us on the new hydro-electric grid rather than the local diesel generators. This should be done by the end of November. This huge transformer was brought here from Mombasa by "Interfreight", the same company which is bringing my containers. By the way, I got through to Interfreight in Nairobi by phone a couple of days ago and found out that my 2 containers arrived in Mombasa last week. Mr. Hans Blassberg, who is the general manager, projected that they should be in Shinyanga in about 2 or 3 weeks' time. I have the foundations built where the containers will sit.

It has been dry for about 2 weeks now and so I was able to drive up here the short way which saves about 50 miles and 2 hours of bad road. The total driving time is 6 hours rather than 8.

I had a nice chat with Fr. (Dr.) Bill Fryda last night. He is taking a refresher course here in Kiswahili. He gave me a picture of the 3 of us (Sr. Leonarda, you, and I) taken in Sioux Falls when we attended his first mass, which I am sending on to Sr. Leonarda.

Peace and love,

Fr. Marvin

Footnote:

Dr. Bill Fryda started out as a lay missionary in Tanzania. After finishing his 3 year commitment as a lay missionary, he decided to enter the seminary. After his ordination in 1988, my aunt, Sr. Leonarda, my sister, Dorothy, and I attended his first solemn mass in Sioux Falls, South Dakota.

Queen of Peace Youth Center
P.O. Box 47, Shinyanga
Tanzania

Nov. 7, 1988

Dear Dorothy,

Many thanks for your letter of Oct. 11. I am happy to hear that Joan Barron sent the money for the cloth I bought for her display in Nairobi. I guess Dennis Kluge isn't going to cash the check I sent him. He's a very nice guy and probably doesn't want any reimbursement for the great help he wants to give us. He is the one who has agreed to come to help put in the electricity in all the buildings. I called Ed Wortman last week by phone. Dennis Kluge and Bill Hess still are intent on coming. I told them to come around January 10th and I will meet them. By that time I will have the housing ready for them.

I have some very good news. The containers arrived on Oct. 26. The driver came at 7:30 in the morning and said my two containers were about a block away. He had gotten lost and was looking around for the center. We had everything from both containers unloaded by 3:30 P.M. I have 10 workers coming here every day and with all that help

---

it didn't take a long time. I went to see the Italian who is working on the hydroelectric towers and he agreed to send his crane whenever we were ready. The crane came at 4 P.M. and both containers were eased down on The driver left immediately for Mwanza which is 90 miles away. He had a very fast trip and had no trouble at any place including customs at the Kenya, Tanzania border which is quite remarkable. He had to pay no bribes and was allowed to go right through.

Joan Baron's container which went out 3 weeks before mine, still has not arrived, perhaps because her papers were not made out right. Nothing in my containers was broken or lost. I have all my tools set up. The table saw and the plainer work terrific. The router is quite and instrument. I am working on a hutch for the dishes in the kitchen. It looks professional with the fancy wood designs you can do with a router. Also I have the 5 by 8 rugs in place in the sitting room, perfect size and color.

So I have a lot to be thankful for. Fr. Dick Hochwalt said, "Our Blessed Mother is watching over you." I believe that myself.

Thanks for your prayers, A very happy thanksgiving.
Much love ,
Fr. Marvin

Footnote:

It was quite remarkable how quickly the two containers arrived. (Oct. 26) I got the news that they arrived at the port city of Mombasa in Kenya. I wanted to go to Nairobi in Kenya on a shopping trip but didn't want to go if the containers were going to arrive. I had to be at the youth center when they came. I got a call through to Hans Blasberg in Nairobi and asked him when he thought they would arrive in Shinyanga. He said it would be between 2 and three weeks for the 900 mile trip. I decided that I had time to go to Nairobi (600 miles) and still make it back in plenty of time. However, the very next day, about 7:30 in the morning, there was a knock on my door. It was the driver of the truck who announced that my 2 containers were here. I couldn't believe it. He said he made the 900 mile trip in 4 days, record time. He had got through the border crossing in a flash. No delay, looking for bribes, etc. It had never happened before and I don't think it will ever happen again.

I told the driver where to park and we would unload the containers. We put most of the stuff in the library building. I went to see the Italian working on the water project who had promised to help me with his crane to off-load the containers on to the foundations we had built. The whole operation went like clock-work. At 4 P.M. he arrived with his crane. It was truly remarkable.

That night thieves tried to break into the library to get at the contents of the container. My dog, Blackie, chased them away. I knew we had to have bars put into the windows to make them burglar proof. That would be done too in a remarkable way as you will see.

I should say a few words about my dog, Blackie. He was a wonderful dog. He was one of the 10 puppies of Doto, the dog that gave birth in the abandoned chicken house at Shinyanga Secondary School a few years back while I was in the U.S. on leave; and who died when the puppies were only about a month old from poison. These little puppies got to know me very well because I fed them until they were old enough to be given away. I had given Blackie to Edward, the watchman at the Bishop's residence right across the way from the Queen of Peace Youth Center. When I moved into the youth center residence in October of 1988, Blackie came right over and refused to leave my house. Edward got very angry and came over with a stick and beat the dog and forced it to go back home. Well, Blackie wouldn't stay there. Beating or not, he kept coming over to my place. I finally convinced Edward to let Blackie stay with me and he agreed. I don't think I ever had a dog that I liked more than Blackie. He was a wonderful watch dog and companion. He was faithful to the end. He was poisoned a couple of years later by thieves who threw tainted meat over the fence at night.

Queen of Peace Youth Center
P.O. Box 47, Shinyanga
Tanzania

Sunday, Dec. 4, 1988

Merry Christmas

Dear Dorothy,

Many thanks for your letter of Nov. 9. No doubt you were quite surprised when Fran Lamosse called you a few days ago. She had written to me about 6 weeks ago asking if she could come here with her son, Roger. I thought it over quite a while and finally called to tell her it would be O.K. because a letter just wouldn't get to her in time. I think it will work out fine. My big concern is having enough living accommodations for 2 extra people. Also, Brother Kevin Dargan, who is supposed to come here to live and work, will probably come about the same time, mid-January. He has been on sabbatical leave.

We are making good progress with the offices which they can use as living quarters when they come. They are now painted and the windows have been reinforced with iron bars. There is no electricity out there, but I plan to run a cord out there connected to my house so each one can have a lamp in the evening. Also I have an extra shower and toilet set up now which is in a building real close to where they will be staying, so I think it will all work out and be a lot of fun. I even have my automatic washing machine working which will be a tremendous help for everybody's laundry. We built a special small tank (out of a barrel) which is just above the machine. Otherwise the machine wouldn't work most of the time because the water pressure in the town system is off most of the day. The tank fills up at night and can handle about 2 loads of clothes.

All those things in the containers are really helpful. Remember we talked about the heavy iron wire mesh for the *big auditorium windows? It is even stronger than iron bars and is saving a tremendous amount of work. We have started to put it in. It will also save me two weeks of time which reinforcing the huge windows with iron bars would have taken.*

I have my altar set up now in our small chapel where I now have daily mass. The altar cloths are tremendous. I am working on the tabernacle which is almost ready. Just the varnishing is left and we will soon have the Blessed Sacrament reserved.

I wrote to Ed Wortman telling him that you can write a check if needed to pay for the airline ticket for Dennis Kluge and Bill Hess. It will cost at least $5000. I would prefer to pay later when I can pay everything at once, but if they need their own money now, you can write a check from my account. Fran and her son, Roger, are going to pay their own way. Ed's telephone number in Hill city is: 1 – 218 697 2763.

I want to wish you, Margaret and Deb, a very blessed and joyful Christmas, with much love.
Fr. Marvin

Footnote:

To get back to my story - Dennis Kluge, Bill Hess and Fran Lamosse, had all agreed to come to Tanzania in January of 1989 to help me with the finishing of the Youth Center. Fran Lamosse's son, Roger, also wrote that he was coming with his mother. He said he was a welder and like his mother, would pay his own way over and back. I wasn't so sure about Roger. He was about 40 years old, lived with his girlfriend, didn't go to church etc. But since he said he was coming and wouldn't take no for an answer, there wasn't much I could do about it. All were coming on a Tourist visa which meant they would not need work permits from the Tanzanian government.

I drove to Nairobi in my double cab pickup around January 8th. I expected my four guests to arrive one day apart. Dennis and Bill were coming together on one flight to arrive on Tuesday. Fran and her son, Roger on another flight, due to arrive on Wednesday morning. Dennis and Bill missed their flight from Frankfurt to Nairobi because they didn't understand that the flight was being called over the loudspeaker for boarding. Thus they were delayed one day. Fran and Roger's flight was right on time and I was there at the Nairobi airport to meet them. Roger was dressed like one of Hell's angels. He had on a tank T- shirt, black leather jacket, boots and long hair. I could see from that moment that he would be a challenge. We finally all were together at the Nairobi Maryknoll house on Wednesday afternoon. There was excitement in the air. Everyone was raring to go. And so - on to my next letter to Dorothy:

Nairobi

Thursday, Jan. 12, 1989

Dear Dorothy,

I want to get a few words off to you before we all leave for down-country to let you know that everything is o.k. Dennis Kluge and Bill Hess got delayed. They were not on the scheduled flight which was on Tuesday. I was at the airport to meet them but no show. They missed a connecting flight through some misunderstanding and then arrived yesterday, Wednesday. Fran and her son, Roger came on schedule, Wednesday morning. Anyhow, they are all here and we plan to leave this afternoon and go as far as Molo, a 4 hour drive. Molo is in the highlands, a very beautiful spot, an elevation 8000 ft., and so it is very nice and cool there. There is an old hotel there with fireplaces in the rooms. It will be a nice place to spend the night before heading down to Tanzania. One of Dennis' bags was lost. We are going to the airport this morning to see if it has been found. Other than that, everything is o.k.

Enclosed is a check from Rosy (Rosmer) Hall for my account.

Love,
Fr. Marvin

Footnote:

Since I have no record of further letters to my sister Dorothy until Feb. 7, I will continue with my recollections. On our way down to the Tanzanian border, I remember passing through a small town in Kenya. All of a sudden I hear Fran say in an excited voice, "Stop the car, stop the car!" I stopped immediately thinking something was wrong, Roger jumped out of the car and ran up to a small shop (called a "duka" in Kiswahili). Fran cried out, "Roger is having a nicotine fit". He came back with a whole carton of cigarettes (Sportsman brand). I remembered that Roger told me that when I picked him up at the Nairobi airport that he was going to reform his life. For one thing he was going to give up smoking. I noticed that the fingers on his right hand were yellow from nicotine which indicated that he was a heavy smoker. To give up smoking "cold turkey" is easier said than done. If Roger was to give up smoking, it would not happen in Africa, that became clear.

We all arrived safely at the Youth center. Each one had a room in the office block. We ran extension cords from my house so that each one would have light. I was surprised to see Brother Kevin Dargan living in the house when we arrived. He had been home on leave in the U.S. He was assigned to help me to teach religion in the high schools. I had requested of our regional superior, Fr. Ed Hayes, that Brother Kevin did not come until we finished the construction since there would not be much for him to do until my guests had left and we would be free to start our apostolate. Brother Kevin liked to cook. Fran Lamosse took over the kitchen as was agreed upon. We had a conflict there and finally I had to give each one of them a turn to avoid complications.

We arrived on Saturday afternoon. The next day, Sunday, I had mass in a room adjoining the library. After mass and breakfast, Dennis Kluge wanted to see all the electrical supplies that had come in the container and had been stored in the library. He then wanted to look up in the attic of the classroom block and so I showed him the trap door in the ceiling. He went up there and then asked Bill Hess to throw up a spool of wiring. I thought he just wanted to look around, but no, he was already stringing the wiring from room to room. I had told him that Sunday was not a day of work. But he was so anxious to get going that he couldn't wait until Monday. All he said after a couple of hours up there was that there were a lot of bats up there. From that moment on, I knew that Dennis and Bill would have everything done in one month.

Father Marv (left) discusses an electrical problem with Dennis Kluge (right) as Bill Hess looks on.

Fran LaMosse and some Tanzanian workers take a break.
Her son, Roger LaMosse, is second from right.

Because of my guest workers, the work progressed amazingly fast. I hired two young African men to help Dennis Kluge. They were very interested in learning the American way of installing electricity. Instead of wires on poles, Dennis buried under ground all the cables between the buildings. These two young men became excellent electricians as a result of this training and did many more jobs for me and for the diocese as time went on.

Roger (pictured above, second from the right) turned out to be a very big asset to the project. He was very creative in finding new ways to make a building burglar proof. He used reinforcing rods on the windows, making them into designs instead of straight iron bars . (see example in picture on the next page).

Bishop Castor Sekwa, who lived only a couple of hundred yards away from the youth center, came almost every day to see the progress. He said to me that the speed in which things were being accomplished would not be possible without your American workers.

Bill Hess was truly a jack of all trades. It seemed like there was nothing that he couldn't do. He turned my two containers into two little houses, cutting in doors and windows, and putting an elevated roof on top to make them cooler. He also paneled one of them with the 4x8 panel sheets that I had sent over in the containers. Bill and Dennis worked about 10 hours a day and enjoyed every minute of it. Their African experience was so unique. The whole operation turned out to be a perfect fit. Again, I have to say that our Blessed Mother had a great deal to do with it. I asked the bishop whether we could rename the center, Queen of Peace Youth Center instead of Charles Luwanda Center. He not only agreed but said that he would have liked to have named his new Cathedral, which was in the planning stage, the same name, but could not because that name had already been taken by another parish. The whole project was becoming very exciting. Mission impossible was turning out to be very possible indeed.

Note the windows in the background. These give you a very good idea of the artistic talent of Roger Lamosse. The primary purpose of the steel mesh and bars in the windows was to keep out thieves. Roger turned them into a work of art. The figures, which need no explanation, are representations of Jesus as King and Mary as queen.

I am pictured with the youth from the Junior College in Shinyanga. I taught a couple of classes a week there. The above were members of the Young Christian Students' organization, among the best youth I ever worked with.

Note my dog, Blackie. Blackie was always around but would never hurt anybody who belonged there.

The remainder of the work went very well. I had promised Bill Hess and Dennis Kluge that I would take them out to the Serengeti plains for a hunting expedition after the work was finished. It just so happened that we had a parish in the Musoma diocese which was way out there near the Serengeti Plains. (Mugumu Parish). Frs. Brian Barrons and Don Larmore were both out there and welcomed me to bring my guests. They said that they were permitted by the government to kill six animals a week to help feed the young boys and girls who were studying at the technical school they had started. It was a wonderful experience for Bill and Dennis to see so many animals and to be able to shoot a few. The game warden actually went with us so we didn't have to worry about breaking any laws for this was not the time for hunting and of course Bill and Dennis did not have licenses.

Mugumu Parish

Monday, Feb. 7, 1989

Dear Dorothy,

I am writing this letter from Mugmuu Parish which is probably our most remote mission station and which borders on the Serengeti Plains, the biggest game reserve in the world. I brought Dennis and Bill here on Saturday, Feb. 5. It is about an 8 hour trip by road from Shinyanga. The reason for coming here is kind of a reward for all the good work they did at the youth center. They wanted to see the animals of the

Serengeti. It turned out better than I had hoped. Not only did they see the animals but also shot a few. The two priests here Brian Barrons and Don Larmore, took us out hunting yesterday. We spent most of the day in their 4-wheel drive vehicle bouncing across the plains chasing tope, impala, gazelle, etc. trying to get close enough for Dennis and Bill to take shots. We ended up with 6 animals and a guinea fowl. Most of the meat will be used by the school here although we enjoyed some delicious gazelle fillets last night.

The work at the youth center went very well. Bill and Dennis are terrific workers. I got everything done that I had hoped for. The center is now completely electrified - a first class job. I gave Bill all the difficult jobs which I would have had to do, like cutting out the doors and windows of the steel containers, putting on the roof, etc. He was equal to every task and amazed the Africans with the speed he worked. The bishop came by almost every day to see the progress and was so pleased that he invited the whole crew back to work on his cathedral when it reaches that stage of completion.

Fran and Roger stayed behind. They want to stay for the opening on April 15th. Roger is a very good welder and finished most of the windows. He is welding an iron frame which fits on the outside of the window frame which will make it very difficult for thieves to break in. Fran took over the kitchen and did all the dishes and kept the house clean. Her contribution was very important especially with the additional mouths to feed.

Nairobi

Thursday, Feb. 9, 1989

We drove from Mugumu to Musoma - about a 4 hour trip - on Tuesday afternoon. The trip took 6 hours because of trouble with my pickup. About an hour out from the mission we heard a grinding noise in the rear. I stopped the vehicle and we discovered the plug at the bottom of the differential had gotten loose and fallen out, and thus all the oil had leaked out. We walked back about a quarter of a mile to see if we could find the plug, but to no avail. A man came by who was a new Christian named Moses. He was very friendly and told us not to worry for he could fix it. He made a wooden plug for us to fill the hole. I happened to have a half liter of engine oil in the car and so we put that in. It was enough lubrication to stop the grinding noise so we took off for Musoma. We stayed at the guest quarters (called the brown house) next to the language school. The next morning at 6:15 AM we left for Nairobi stopping at Kisii in Kenya to get a new plug and the proper No. 90 oil. It took a whole liter and a half to fill the differential. Everyone is telling me how lucky I am that the differential didn't burn out.

This morning Dennis and Bill bought wood carvings etc. to bring home to friends. There are a lot of good things to buy at the Nairobi market at reasonable prices. They leave tonight for the States. I will take them to the airport at 10 PM. They will mail this letter to you in the States.

> *I couldn't say mass for Wally on the 7th but will do so on Saturday, Feb. 11, the feast of Our Lady of Lourdes. I will be here in Nairobi 5 or 6 days before heading down country. I hope all goes well with you.*
>
> *Love,*
> *Fr. Marvin*

Footnote:

A funny thing happened at the airport. - When Bill shot the large antelope and we got back to the mission at Mugumu, he asked if it would be o.k. to bring the antlers back to the U.S. Fr. Barrons told him that this was illegal without a permit and so Fr. Barrons went to see the game warden who had gone out hunting with us to make out a permit. The game warden typed something out and stamped it. Bill spent quite a bit of time boiling all the flesh out of the antlers before we left Mugumu mission. When we got to the airport in Kenya, I was a bit worried that the customs official would not allow Bill to leave with the horns. In fact, he didn't. He asked Bill what he had all wrapped up with string and paper. Bill told him that he had antlers from Tanzania. When I saw the problem, I went over to talk to the customs official. The customs official demanded to see the permit. Bill showed him this piece of paper poorly typed with many mistakes. The customs official thought they were fraudulent. I explained to him that the game warden typed it out, but we in Tanzania do not have good equipment since we are not as advanced as you people in Kenya. The customs official laughed and said to Bill. It's ok. You can take them with you. When Bill got home to Hill

City he mounted the antlers in his living room and was so proud to tell people where he had got them.

Nairobi

Feb. 15, 1989

Dear Dorothy,

After lunch I will be leaving Nairobi for Tanzania. Fr. Carroll Houle is going that way too so we will go together in separate vehicles. He has agreed to carry some of my things. I have paint and parquet floor tiling which is on the heavy side. He will bring the stuff as far as Musoma.

By now Bill Hess and Dennis Kluge are back home in Hill City. They made a big hit out here making repairs at the various places we stopped.

I got a routine checkup by the doctor while I was here - blood, stool, urine test etc. Everything is normal. I had a good rest too.

Enclosed is a check from Fr. George Cotter for my account. I paid Bill and Dennis with checks from my account. All this will be reimbursed by the project money when I present the bills...... This is just a quicky...Regards to all.

Love and prayers,
Fr. Marvin

Queen of Peace Youth Center

P.O. Box 47, Shinyanga
Tanzania

Feb. 28, 1989

HAPPY BIRTHDAY

All that matters is that one is created anew.
~ Gal 6:15

Dear Dorothy,

Looking at the Calendar I see that your birthday this year comes right after Easter which gives extra meaning to it.

We are having the official opening here on April 3rd which is the feast of the Annunciation transferred from March 25 which was in Lent. We are coming to the end of the big building project although there are many small things to do like putting in extra sidewalks, making cabinets, tables, etc. for the various buildings. I am pretty happy with the progress. Brother Kevin and the staff worker I hired, Charles Ngambaseni, finished setting up the library today. The containers are all painted now and fully equipped with electricity. I made a bed today for the one which will be the guest house. Fran wants to move in there tomorrow and spend her last month in there.

Her son, Roger, is helping with various projects. He finished the chapel floor today putting down the 3rd coat of varnish on the parquet wooden floor which he put in. He also welded another security steel frame for one of the windows. He could easily finish them all if we had enough materials. I could have used about twice as much of that flat iron I bought. We are using every scrap of material here. Nothing is wasted.

Thanks for sending me the statements on interest for the income- tax filing. Sorry to hear that John is out of a job. I will drop a line to Margaret and John.

Time is going by quickly. After the opening, Fran and Roger will be leaving. It has been a good experience for all of us.

Again, best wishes and my love and prayers for your birthday. A blessed and joy filled Easter...
Love and prayers,
Fr. Marvin

The container guest house

Brother Kevin Dargan with auditorium in the background

Our new water tank with classroom block in the background

Holy Week 1989: Students celebrate the opening of the Shinyanga Youth Center.

As soon as the buildings were finished, the youth center had its first use - a retreat for the Young Christian Students during Holy Week of 1989. This retreat is called the Easter Conference. As you can see from the pictures, it was well attended. In the top picture, Brother Kevin is pictured with the students. There were 85 students present for the first Easter conference in the new facilities. I immediately saw that we should build a couple of hostels to house them in the future, a project which I was soon to start. The Easter Conference was the big event of the year. The blessing of the youth center on April 3rd, the transferred feast of the Annunciation, came off very well. It was significant, indeed, that the center be blessed on one of Mary's feast days. All the priests of the diocese were there as well. The mass was held in the auditorium.

Queen of Peace Youth Center
P.O. Box 47 Shinyanga
Tanzania

April 16, 1989
5th Sunday of Easter

Dear Dorothy,

I have your letters of March 1 and 17. Many thanks. I am happy to hear that John found a job. That's good news. It has been a while since I have written. I think the last time was from Nairobi when I brought Fran and Roger up to get their plane. I just wrote to Fran. She would like to come back here and be a lay missionary. I just told her that that is not possible this year. She and Brother Kevin, who is now my assistant, did not hit it off. Kev loves to be in the kitchen and in fact would find it very difficult to live happily without this outlet. Kev has some emotional problems which I think I can cope with, but with Fran here there would be too many cooks and the broth would be spoiled, as the old saying goes. I hope Fran doesn't take it too hard.

The young Christian Students retreat during Holy Week was the first big event here at the youth center. We had 80 youth with about 35 sleeping here. The others lived close enough to go home to sleep. It worked out pretty good. The 2nd big event was the opening on April 3rd. About 300 youth attended and about 75 others - including the Bishop, who had the mass and blessing and about 20 priests, quite a few sisters and the rest lay people. Brother Kevin butchered a cow the day before here on the property with the help of a few assistants. The cow was put in the Bishop's compound across the road the day before. As luck would have it, the cow got loose, breaking the rope around its leg. It took a couple of hours to catch it before it could be slaughtered.

The day itself came off very nice. We had been getting a lot of rain, but on that day the weather was perfect. There were about 10 Maryknoll priests here since they came down to attend the opening and then the Maryknoll board meeting which was held here and which began the next day. We put up 5 Maryknollers here and fed all 12 of the board members. This place is terrific for meetings since we have ample space, toilets etc.

We plan to invite the youth from the neighboring high schools to begin using the auditorium and library this week. We have two ping-pong tables, a dart board, card tables and checkers set up in the auditorium. We will begin slowly.

I expect three electric cooking pots, a video, and 10 sewing machines sometime before July. As time goes by we will be able to have the youth stay here conveniently when we build the two hostels. The cooking stoves will be electric and each one will handle one big pot. The sewing machines are the foot-pedal type and are coming from Taiwan since they are no longer made in Europe. We plan to start a sewing class for unemployed girls.

I Plan to drive to Nairobi again in early May with Fr. Dick Hochwalt. I can make my annual retreat there and also pick up some video parts. Our VCR is not working. There is a guy in town who knows how to fix them (he was trained in Japan) but he doesn't have the spares.

We had heavy rains - about 15 inches in one month. About 4 days ago the winds suddenly shifted and now it is sunny, hot and dry. That's o.k. by me. We have our new water tank filled. The roads need to dry out too.

Hope all goes well. I will write from Nairobi.
Love and prayers,
Fr. Marvin

Nairobi

Monday, May 8, 1989

Dear Dorothy,

I am here in Nairobi at the Society house to make my annual retreat. I drove up with Fr. Dick Hochwalt. It is now dry in Tanzania which made it an easy trip. It is raining every day, however, in Nairobi. In fact, it just started to sprinkle a few minutes ago. There will be about 20 making the retreat, 6 of us from the Tanzanian region and 14 from the Kenyan. Fr. John Meehan, whom I knew very well in the seminary going way back to the College days at Glen Ellyn, is giving the retreat. John flew in from Korea where he has been working for many years. The retreat starts tonight after supper.

The work at the youth center was going very well when I left. Every day more youth were coming to use the recreational and library facilities. Over a hundred came one day as the idea is catching on in the neighborhood and nearby schools.

We started to put in a tennis court which can also be used for a volleyball court. We are using clay rather than cement since clay is very inexpensive, and also tennis is something new. Before making it permanent, it is good to see if the youth are attracted to it. I think it will work out. There was just enough space for a tennis court. Now all the property is being used. I still want to put up a garage and a carpenter shop. I also have cabinets and shelving to make. That's the reason for not going to the U.S. next summer. I would like to complete these jobs. As I see it now, it would be better to come next year rather than this, but we will see.

Hope all goes well...
Love and prayers,
Fr. Marvin

Footnote:

There was an empty lot next to the youth center property which unbeknown to me, really belonged to the youth center. The diocesan lay people had taken this over without the permission of the government because they wanted to build a hotel in order to make money. They didn't get the grant to put up the hotel and so when the Bishop told me this, I asked to take this plot over so we could build a basketball court and 2 hostels on it. The Bishop agreed.

Queen of Peace Youth Center

Sunday, Aug. 13, 1989

Athi River

Dear Dorothy,

I am writing this letter from the parish house in Athi River, which is about 25 miles outside of the city of Nairobi. My classmate, Fr. Tom Donnelly is the pastor there, having taken over about 6 months ago from an Irish priest who retired recently - age 76. I arrived in Nairobi on Saturday, Aug. 5 with Fr. Doug Venne who has finished his work in Bangladesh and is visiting Tanzania and Kenya before returning to the U.S. Doug has been assigned to the promotion department. Perhaps he will be assigned to the Minneapolis house. Doug worked with me there in 1969 while he was recuperating from his jeep accident in the Philippines where he lost an eye.

I had quite a few things to do in Nairobi. I brought our VCR up for repair. It is O.K. now. I picked it up yesterday from the shop. I bought a portable Honda generator which I will be able to use for my power tools and also at night for a few lights - and even keep our deep freeze cold if the power is off for an extended period. There has been a lot of trouble with the electricity in Shinyanga. The transformer at the new power station which receives power from the hydroelectric dam many miles away, burned out. Now the town is back on the old diesel generators which are very inadequate. Thus, we only have electricity now and then. It usually comes on in the late evening and is off again in the morning. Except for keeping the fridge working it is not of much use to us.

I plan to leave tomorrow afternoon and go part way on my trip back to Tanzania. I still have the export papers for the generator to pick up from "Lifeline" which is getting all the bank clearances etc. I came to Athi River yesterday afternoon to see Tom Donnelly, my classmate. I will take one of the masses for him this morning and drive back to Nairobi after lunch. Beginning today, Kenya is celebrating its 100th anniversary of the arrival of the first Catholic missionaries, so there are special reading for today's mass.

I hope your trip to Yankton worked out nicely. Yesterday I said mass for the newly-weds, Marybeth and Dale and will do the same next Saturday for Cathy and Mike. By next Sunday I hope to be back at the youth center. I have a budget meeting to attend in Musoma on Wednesday and Thursday.

Enclosed are 2 checks, $25 and $5 which I received for my birthday. Also - a couple of pictures of my garage-carpenter shop which is now finished. I put it up in less than 6 weeks using a wood frame and imported siding. As you can see it fits in very well and part of the garage acts as a backstop for the clay tennis court which is also new. The small building with the 4 doors on the right is the outdoor toilet.

I still want to put up 2 dormitories. I found out that the plot on the other side of the garage belongs to the youth center (which surprised me). That plot is a perfect place for the dormitories since it is close to the toilets. There is also room there for a basketball court. Brother John Walsh, a Maryknoller who is an architect working for the city council in Nairobi, is doing the drawings for me for the dormitories, so they will be according to code. There is still sufficient funds in the project money for the dorms since I saved so much doing the contracting myself.

Love and prayers,

Fr. Marvin

Footnote:

The amount of money left over after the project was completed was quite remarkable, $50,000. With the $150,000 grant from Maryknoll, we not only finished the original plan of 5 buildings, but also put up a huge water tank, cement tennis and basketball courts, a large outdoor toilet and 2 hostels. The Indian contractor said he could not even finish the original 5 buildings with this amount and wanted $225,000. The $50,000 left over was sent up to Sr. Paul Mary in Musoma diocese for the purchase of a new piece of land there for her youth center. My trip to Medjugorje paid off in so many ways. We really felt the help of Mary, Queen of Peace.

Brother Kevin supervising the cooking at the Youth Center opening on April 3

The finished garage and carpenter shop behind the tennis court (outdoor toilet - partially visible)

Fr. Marvin in his workshop making furniture

Queen of Peace Youth Center
P.O. Box 47, Shinyanga
Tanzania

Sunday, Sept. 10, 1989

Dear Dorothy,

Seems like quite a while since I have written. Thanks for your letters of July 12 and Aug. 1. Sounds like you have had a busy summer with all the weddings, visit to Yankton, etc. I hope your trip to visit the sisters in Yankton came off well. I am sure you will describe your trip in your next letter.

Brother John Wohead is back from the U.S. I had asked him if he could bring a 1000 gallon steel water tank down from Musoma on his way back. Brother John had left his pickup in Nairobi and since he was coming back empty, I had asked him if he could pick up the tank in Musoma on his way down . His pick-up is big enough to carry it. I am grateful to him for his help. We have a 6000 gallon cement tank which gets water off the roof of the auditorium. The 1000 gal tank is for the house. I'll be putting up the gutters for that this week. We got our first rain of the season this past week (total 3/4 inch) which is a big help. The water pressure from the town supply is usually very low and dirty. Rain water is so much better and with our tanks we can make it. Almost all the trees we planted survived the dry season. They should really take off this year, which will make the place very attractive.

Now that the carpenter shop and garage are finished and my workbench and tools are set up, I have hired a carpenter, a man who lives nearby who said he worked here years ago when the construction first started. He seems to be o.k. and I have plenty for him to do making pallets for our block-making machine. The pallets are boards 9" by 6" by 9". The cement is placed in the pallet.and put on the ground to partially dry. When the cement block is hardened, the pallet is removed and used over again. We will begin soon to make cement blocks. I think I mentioned in my last letter that I discovered that the plot north of us is youth center property and thus we have plenty of space to put up 2 hostels and a basketball court. There is still money left over from the original grant which should be sufficient for the completion of these additions.

I have been teaching this term, but just two classes a week, one at Shinyanga Commercial School and one at Buluba Secondary School. We have quite a bit of help for the teaching with Brother Kevin here as well as Charles Gambaseni, our librarian and staff member, plus 2 former seminarians who are also helping out. Till next time...

With love and prayers,
Fr. Marvin

Maryknoll Society House
Dares Salaam

Monday, Oct. 9, 1989

Dear Dorothy,

I am writing this letter from Dar es Salaam. I came here by Mwadui Mines plane on Thursday, Oct. 5 to pick up the video, VCR and 3 cookers for the youth center. I plan to leave tomorrow for Shinyanga in Fr. Zachary's (African Father from Shinyanga diocese) new double-cab pickup which is just like mine. He is happy that I am driving it to Shinyanga for him and I am happy to use it to bring some of my stuff down.

Just before I came to Dar we started the sewing class for 16 young girls. Paula Eingeman, the wife of the Swiss lay missionary teaching mechanics, is teaching the girls. As you know, the Swiss are very good at sewing and detail work, so I know they will receive a good training. Paula wants the girls to do only hand sewing first and later on to learn how to use the machines. The 10 sewing machines which were part of the same order as the cookers and video, arrived earlier in a different shipment since they came from Taiwan. They were completely disassembled. It took me a good half day to get the first one put together, but after getting one set up, the rest were easy. They are the old fashion foot pedal type and do not have the zig-zag stitch, but plenty good for our purpose.

Before I left for Dar, our workers had about 1000 cement blocks made for the new hostels. The plans have been submitted to the city council and I expect the approval by the time I return, so I think we will be able to break ground in about a week's time.

> *Thanks for your last letter written on Sept. 10 which I received before coming to Dar. Sorry to hear that Margaret has to look for a new job. I am praying that all will turn out well for her.*
>
> *F. John Lange has been to the house twice while I am here in Dar, which was very nice. The house is in real good shape and just about as nice as when John and I were here. Fr. Howie O'Brien, the new procurator, is doing a real good job here and is very hospitable.*
>
> *I hope this letter gets to you a little sooner than usual. It should since it is being mailed in Dar. My greetings to Deb...*
>
> *Love and prayers,*
> *Fr. Marvin*

The following picture is my crew who were building the hostels (dormitories) - and a few months later when finished. - in the lower picture, you can see the backstop of the basketball court.

Queen of Peace Youth Center

Sunday, Nov. 12, 1989

Dear Dorothy,

Thanks very much for your letter of Oct. 13. I am happy to hear that the St. Helena's festival turned out so well. It is surprising how much money they made.

Today I am taking one of the masses at the town parish which begins at 10 AM which gives me about a half hour to write a few lines. Late afternoon yesterday, we had a nice rain of about 3/4 of an inch. There had been no rain at all since Sept, so we were very happy to see it come. It has been so hot and dusty. Our trees and flowers are doing pretty well even without the rain since we have a yard boy who waters every other day. But now the grass will grow too. Mohans, a Danish fellow about 50, is working on the tennis court right now, scraping and rolling the clay base. He comes now and then for a game and does more than his share in keeping the court in shape. His wife likes to play too and often comes with him.

Last Tuesday, Wednesday and Thursday we had a meeting here for all the Maryknoll priests, brothers and lay people of Shinyanga diocese. Altogether there were 20 of us. It was kind of a pre-chapter meeting. Even though our chapter will not be held until October of 1990, we are getting a head start. We only had two priests staying with us. The others found housing at the lay mission house in town and at Buhangija, where there are lots of rooms - located about a mile outside of town. We had all the meals here. About 5 of the local girls and boys helped us with the serving and dishwashing. The girls are from the sewing course which is going on in the morning. We had all the meals outside on the patio. The trees and bushes you can see in the pictures I sent you are much bigger now, giving enough shade. The set up here is very good for meetings.

On Friday afternoon we showed the new film on AIDS which has been produced by the government. Dr. Mawazo, the coordinator for the AIDS project has asked for our cooperation since we have good facilities here and a 16 mm projector. Seems like all the projectors in town are broken down. AIDS is becoming a very serious problem in Tanzania, much more so, I think, than in the U.S., since it attacks both men and women in equal numbers. We are all helping to get the news out to the school children and towns people.

The building of the hostels is going along well. The foundations are now in on the first one. In a couple of weeks we will have all the walls up. I have about 10 workers coming every day....It's time to go to the town parish for mass so will close for now...

Greetings to all...Love,
Fr. Marvin

The graduation day of the sewing class

Students with Fr. Richard Duffy

The sewing classes which Paula Eingenen started caught on very quickly. Prisla Lugohe replaced Paula when Paula returned to Switzerland. Each course was about 3 months. The students first learned hand sewing and then how to use the machines. This became standard procedure. The first picture is graduation day for the class. Prisla is the person facing me with her arm outstretched.

In the second picture, the class is showing off their work. Fr. Richard Duffy, my Franciscan friend from College days was visiting that day.

The third is graduation day for another group who finished a follow up course.

Among the above 3 pictures, the top picture was taken shortly after the center was opened in 1989. The middle picture is the same house several years later when the trees and bushes had matured. The lower picture is the fully furnished container guest house which even had electricity, a bathroom and running water supplied by a tank on the roof.

The picture below is of the auditorium when it was used for the first time for the Easter conference in 1989. There were no trees.

Holy Week 1989: Students celebrate the opening of the Shinyanga Youth Center.

The following two pictures were taken a few years later. It was amazing how fast the trees grew.

The Patio was where we served the food. In the above picture there is a shelter on the left which was put in by Bill Hess (the master builder from Minnesota) I planted the trees - Ficus Benjamin type which do not shed their leaves hoping we would have a shady place for many to sit, especially while eating.

As you can see from these two pictures, they grew magnificently. The picture above is of the library (from the

283

same perspective as the above picture on top these two except closer up). We put the statue of our Lady surrounded by bougainvillea in front of the library window. You can see the statue in both pictures if you look closely.

For 25 years I taught religion in high schools and Junior Colleges. This, perhaps, was the most challenging of all my work in Tanzania. Fortunately, religion was part of the curriculum. However, often times we received the worst periods - early afternoon.

I think I should say a few words about Brother Kevin. Brother Kevin was intelligent and had an excellent memory. He loved books and specialized in history. He put together an excellent library which he codified. He also taught many classes in the secondary schools and for the most part was well liked. We were opposites in temperament and personality. It didn't take much to make him angry. As for myself, it took quite a lot. Perhaps that is why we lasted 6 years together at the youth center.

The top picture is of our two vehicles. We both had double cab Toyota pickups. Mine was white and his was green. With the help of our carpenter, we designed wooden enclosures for the back of the pickups which could be locked up safeguarding whatever we were carrying from thieves and keeping out the rain and dust.

Chapter IV

Bishop Castor Sequa asks that I build the Priest's hostel and the diocesan office block

I would like to call this section of my book "Letters from Africa - Mission Impossible Revisited". To build the unfinished Youth Center was the first mission impossible achieved. I am convinced that it would not have been completed without the help of our Blessed Mother and the grace of God. What happened next in my mind fluctuates between a nightmare and amazement at the continual help of God in our mission work.

After the work on the youth center was completed, I thought I could settle down to the routine of running the Youth Center and teaching the religion courses in the 3 Secondary Schools in the area and in the Commercial School in Shinyanga town (equivalent to a Junior College) But fate and the Bishop, Castor Sekwa, had different plans for me, which although quite successful, were very detrimental to my overall health and wellbeing.. I did things I never dreamed I would ever be called upon to do. The following pages tell the story which I have been somewhat reluctant to tell, but after thinking it over and praying about it, decided that "Letters from Africa" would not be complete without relating the last part of my mission career.

A little background - Bishop Castor Sekwa had high ambitions on setting up a permanent diocesan center in a section of Shinyanga town called Ngokolo. Previously, under Maryknoll Bishop, Edward McGurkin, the diocesan headquarters had been established at Buhangija, located about a mile outside of town on the road to Tabora. Bishop

Sekwa was consecrated Bishop in 1975 and continued to function out of Buhangija. However, everyone knew that this was not ideal, especially as the diocese began to develop with the number of Catholics and local priests increasing dramatically. The Bishop received a large piece of land equivalent to almost 2 square blocks, on the edge of Shinyanga town, a section called Ngokolo. I don't know the exact date that he received the land, but it was some time, I believe, in the early 1980's.

A master plan was developed which I think was a good one. On the largest section- the Bishop's house, a cathedral, a hostel for the priests, diocesan offices, a convent with an adjoining kindergarten school, would be built. On the other section, across the street - a youth center and dispensary would be built. In 1988 when I entered the scene to work on the Youth Center, the Bishop's house was complete, the work on the Cathedral was well underway, and the Sisters' Convent and adjoining nursery school, were progressing nicely. In April of 1989, after the youth center was blessed and was functioning very well, the Bishop wanted to move on to new construction. He wanted to build the 22 bedroom priests' hostel and the diocesan offices close to the hostel. He said he didn't have enough money to hire a contactor. He asked a couple of the Maryknoll Brothers to act as contractor, but they refused saying that they had enough to do without taking on such a major project.

And so the Bishop came to me. He had seen how the Youth Center, after lying in the weeds for years, was finalized in a very short period of time and functioning very well. The Bishop reasoned - if Fr. Marvin could do this - couldn't he also supervise the construction of the priests' hostel and diocesan office block? And so the Bishop put quite a bit of pressure on me to do the supervision. He said, "We have a good foreman, Angelo, well trained in construction, who can handle the day to day supervision of the construction. All you have to do is be of assistance to him and keep an eye on the project." He asked me a number of times and each time I refused. I said this is far beyond my expertise. I have no training or schooling in this kind of construction. Anyhow, against my better judgment, I finally agreed and proceeded to help Angelo lay out the footings using knowledge I had learned years earlier from Maryknoller, Brother George Carlonas. And so the construction began. At first it was O.K. I sat down with the Bishop and modified the plans somewhat to put in a dining area on the first phase instead of the second phase which would be a couple of years down the line.

Actually, when it was time for me to go home on leave in 1991, the project was going very well with much of the construction completed. However, most of it was done without Angelo. After only a couple of months into the project, he came down with AIDS. He returned to his home in another part of the country and died about 6 weeks later. Also, although burning the candle at both ends, I had been able to carry out my duties at the youth center and taught in the schools quite satisfactorily. It was only later, after returning from leave and getting involved in the cathedral project that my health began to fail. I don't want to get ahead of my story and so will begin with some letters I had written to my sister, Dorothy.

Queen of Peace Youth Center
P.O.Box 47, Shinyanga
Tanzania

Sunday, Feb. 3, 1991

Dear Dorothy,

Many thanks for your letter of Jan. 13 which arrived on Feb. 1. You mentioned the cold weather. By the time you get this letter, the worst will probably be over. Here we have been having some very good rains - 1 1/2 inches last night. The rice crop is doing well and so is everything else. The past few years have been exceptionally good. Our trees and shrubs are growing like mad. One would think the youth center had been around for 10 years rather than just 2 this Easter.

About a week ago our big dog, "Blackie" got very sick. Seems that he was poisoned by would-be-thieves who must have thrown bad meat over the fence in the middle of the night. Blackie died two days later. We miss him because he was a terrific watchdog. Nobody could come near the place at night without him sounding the alert. We still have 3 smaller dogs (who are all in my office as I write this letter), but they don't have the aggressiveness of Blackie.

The table saw continues to work fine since I am the only one who uses it. I do all the special cutting and never have it on more than 15 minutes at a time so it doesn't heat up. My carpenters have finished about 15 cabinets for the new hostel (we need 22 for the 22 bedrooms) All the inside plastering will be finished in about 2 weeks time so we are making progress.

The war goes on. I had expected a much stronger response from Iraq. I pray every day that it may be over without more loss of life.

Love and prayers,

Fr. Marvin

Footnote:

The Bishop asked me to change the plans somewhat regarding showers. Instead of having just a few for everyone, he wanted a shower attached to each room. This required a big addition to the plumbing arrangement. I had a plumber who was pretty good. He made the switch right away. There were a couple of problems. The biggest one was the lack of water in the town system. There rarely would be enough pressure for the showers to work right. I had to build a cistern to collect the water and then build a water tower. We would then use an electric pump to pump the water up into the tower. I became a good friend of the African who was in charge of putting up the steel girders in the Cathedral close by. He said he could hoist the tank up and place it on the tower. He did this with ease.

One day the plumber told me that his pipe threader had been stolen. What to do now. There weren't any more of these around in town. At 8 A.M. every morning I had a roll call for all my workers which at that time numbered about 15. I reported to the crew that the threader had been stolen. I said I had prayed to our Blessed Mother to get it back again some way.   About a week later, one of the workers at the 8 A.M. roll call said the pipe threader was back. He said he saw it laying in the grass on the other side of the fence across the way at the Bishop's compound. (about a quarter of a block away). I went over there right away and sure enough, there it was, laying in the grass. I found out through the grape vine that the thieves had tried to sell the threader at the cotton store (a place where the cotton crop was baled and stored) about 5 miles away. The man in charge there started to ask questions from the thieves asking them where they got this tool. The thieves got worried thinking that they might get caught and so decided to return the pipe threader. After that, the men began to think that I had magic charms and received special protection from higher powers.

Another problem I had with the workers was the demands of funerals. The African custom demanded that when anyone dies in the village, everyone in the village had to be there for the grieving and mourning which was actually the next day after the death. (Without embalming, the body was usually buried within 24 hours). Because of the AIDS pandemic, many people were dying on a regular basis. Rarely could I count on having a full work force.

There were so many woes connected with building. I will explain more as we progress with the letters.

Queen of Peace Youth Center
P.O. Box 47, Shinyanga
Tanzania

Feb. 24, 1991

Dear Dorothy,

Greetings from Queen of Peace Youth Center. I heard on the BBC a few hours ago that the land war has begun in Kuwait. Our Lady's message to the children at Medjugorje on Jan. 25, 1990 seems to refer to the gulf:

"Dear children, today I am inviting you to pray. May your prayer be for peace. Satan is strong and wishes to destroy not only your human life, but also nature and the planet you live on..."

The youth center continues to be a very busy place. An African priest, Fr. Deo Gratias from Kahama diocese, brought his football team here for a week using our hostels while they played at Kambarage stadium. A group of about 35 building contractors used our hall for a 2 week seminar. This past week, Dr. Mawazo, the AIDS coordinator for Shinyanga district, conducted a seminar here for 45 AIDS counselors, including Protestant pastors, Catholic priests, Moslem leaders and social workers. We have video facilities which are very helpful. There is an excellent video documentary made by Sweden on

---

the pop singer, Philly Lutaya of Uganda who contacted AIDS a few years ago. He spent the rest of his life crusading against it. He died on Dec. 15, 1989. East Africa is called the AIDS belt. There are a million and a quarter with HIV in Uganda and 800,000 in Tanzania.

All is going well here. Our Blessed Lady really takes care of us... A joyful Easter in the risen Christ, the Prince of Peace.

Love and prayers,
Fr. Marvin

P.S. Hi to Deb... If all goes according to plan, I would like to take my home leave about mid-August.

Palm Sunday,
March 24, 1991

Dear Dorothy,
    Thanks for your letters of Jan. 27, Feb. 14 and Feb. 27. The first two took over a month in coming - perhaps because of a hold up as a result of the war. The Feb. 27th letter took 3 weeks which is about normal.

The picture below gives you a good idea on how the priests' hostel is coming along. It is bigger than it looks - 30 rooms. You can't see the left wing very well which is longer than the right ring. We are now putting down the cement floor. The electrical and plumbing is almost finished. There is a lot of finishing to do - painting, furnishing etc. Believe it or not. So far the cost has been only about $50,000. Complete it should be less than $100,000, about $150,000 less than a contractor would have charged.

The office - conference room block is perpendicular to the hostel. The foundation for that is now in. One nice thing as you can see - the trees in between are quite large. We didn't have to cut down a single tree. I plan to put in a patio with outdoor tables and chairs which will make the place very homey - a nice place to sit for get-togethers , retreats, etc.

This is the last big project I will accept. If the Bishop wants help with the cathedral furnishing, I can do that but no more 30 room buildings. The youth center is going very well. Fortunately I have some good help. We have a big group coming for the Holy Week retreat - about a hundred students for meals, 40 of whom will sleep here.

The rains have stopped for almost 3 weeks and the crops are in danger. If we get good rains this week, a lot can be saved, especially the rice crop. I am sure happy that the war is over in Iraq, but peace is a long way off.

Happy springtime......
    With love and prayers,
    Fr. Marvin

Queen of Peace Youth Center
P.O. Box 47, Shinyanga
Tanzania

April 18, 1991

Dear Dorothy,

Today is the second day of a 2 day celebration for the Moslems - the end of the Ramadan fast. I like these holidays - no school or work which gives me a chance to catch up on a few things.

Thank you for your letter of March 10. No doubt another one will come as soon as I mail this. The rains are not so good this year. In my last letter I complained of a dry spell. A couple of days after I wrote we got several inches of rain over a three day period, which was a big help. But then they stopped again (for two and a half weeks) until last night when we got about a half inch. The first two weeks in April are when we ordinarily get heavy rains, so it looks like a poor year for the crops. The property, however, looks good since there has been enough rain for the grass and the trees.

Since I wrote on Palm Sunday, this has been a busy place. We had over 100 youth for the Holy Week retreat, 40 of whom were housed here. They represented 9 schools from as far away as 60 miles.

Last week the Maryknoll Board meeting was held here. There are 10 board members. The only one who couldn't come was Fr. John Lange who would have had to drive 600 miles from Dar. He wasn't feeling good and it's just too far to drive. We used our 2 youth hostels which can be made into 7 private rooms with a recreation room in each hostel. It was a very busy time for me. Brother Kevin is on the board which meant that I had to supervise the kitchen plus my other work.

This Sunday is Vocation Sunday. I have a group of about 20 boys and girls from a neighboring school coming for a 1 day retreat. Hope all goes well with you and Deb and that Steve has found his own place...

Love and prayers,
Fr. Marvin.

Dar es Salaam

May 8, 1991

Dear Dorothy,

Greetings from Dar es Salaam. I arrived here a week ago with Brother Cyril who wanted to come here to pick up his new vehicle. We drove up here in his old one (double cab 4 wheel drive Toyota pickup) which I will drive back. We have spent most of the past week shopping and have done very well. We also have our diocesan 7 ton truck here which was driven up a week earlier by our diocesan driver, Nestori, but he had a breakdown and had to put the truck in the garage. All is O.K. now. The truck is packed with all kinds of building materials that I need to finish the hostel, also medicines for our diocesan dispensaries etc. etc. I was able to get one fridge and one electric stove here in Dar which will fit into the back of the pickup. I have ordered a deep freeze, electric stove and fridge from Sweden which will be coming air-freight in perhaps 6 weeks' time. I am hoping to have the hostel operational by the middle of July which might be possible with the materials we are bringing back.

I hope you are coping with everything there. Seems like life is tough at times, but we have to put our trust in the Lord and place all in the hands of Our Lady.

We hope to leave in a few hours and go as far as Dodoma. Brother Cyril is picking up the fridge right now. He should have gotten it yesterday, but a worker at the duty free shop where we are buying the fridge forgot the key to the bonded warehouse where the packed fridge is stored.

Fr. John Lange was here a couple of times and stayed overnight. The house is being painted again to restore its original appearance. The grounds are in poor shape however, but could be made to look quite nice with a little bit of attention. I am happy to hear you had some summer weather.

With prayers and best wishes,
Love,
Fr. Marvin

Footnote:

A few pages earlier in this book, I mentioned that the building I was doing caused me to have nightmares. This trip was one of them.   I remember very well what happened.

Brother Cyril and I left Dar, driving separately in two pickups.   We started out in the morning about the same time as our driver in the 7 ton truck.   The driver's name was Nestori.   He had been working for Brother Cyril for a long time.   I didn't know him very well. The contents of the truck he was driving were very important to me in order to carry on the work of the hostel. One of the items in the truck was very fragile.   Bishop Sekwa wanted the dining area in the hostel to be special and so ceramic tiles for the floor had been ordered from Italy. I wasn't sure if it was a good idea to bring them to Shinyanga in the 7 ton lorry because the road from Dodoma to Shinyanga, a distance of 300 miles, was so bad.   I was worried that the corrugations and pot holes would shake the truck so badly that many of the tiles would be broken.

The first leg of the trip - Dar to Dodoma - was a piece of cake, at least for Brother Cyril and me.   The distance is about 300 miles and it is all tarmac. Brother Cyril and I got there in the late afternoon. We checked in at the Dodoma diocese center house which is very large and had good guest accommodations. We finished having supper with some of the priests there about 7:30 P.M. which was typical. We were wondering about the 7 ton lorry because it had not yet arrived. Well, the driver, Nestori, appeared on the scene but without the truck. He was quite flustered and reported that he had had an accident about 75 miles back and was fortunate to get a ride from a passing vehicle which brought him to Dodoma. He said that one of the tires blew out as he was coming down a long incline. The truck went off the road and was partially tipped over in a ditch on the side of the road. Thinking about all the valuable materials in the truck, caused us great alarm. Thieves would pilfer any abandoned truck. Nestori said that his assistant was with the truck and would not abandon it. We discussed what we should do, and decided to try to get the aid of one of the local Italian Missionaries who had a big truck. The Italian priest agreed to help, but said it would not be possible to get his truck on the road until the next morning.

The next morning, Brother Cyril, Nestori and I drove to the scene of the accident, followed by the Missionary truck. Our plan was to transfer all the materials into the new truck and try to get our truck upright again, once the load was off. It took almost 2 hours to get there. When we got there we were greatly relieved to discover that Nestori's assistant was there and nothing had been stolen. We pulled the Missionary's truck along side and transferred all the enclosed goods and materials into it. Fortunately our truck had not tipped over completely and with the aid of heavy ropes fastened to the two trucks, we were able to get our truck upright and out of the ditch. I looked at the tires on our truck and saw that they were badly worn. And so I said to Brother Cyril, "how could you permit our truck to travel with tires so badly worn?." Brother Cyril said that he had just replaced the tires recently and they were all new and in good condition.

And so the plot thickens. We found out that the driver Nestori, had sold the new tires. Also that he had been moonlighting with the truck, using it for private deals to make money for himself. He was building a new house and needed the money.

We were very fortunate to get our truck on the road again. If the truck had had the accident a few hundred yards previous, or a few hundred yards later, it would have gone completely over since there was no supporting ditch to hold it up. And so we all went back to Dodoma in all the vehicles, - the Italian Missionary's truck loaded with our stuff, Nestori, driving our diocesan truck after the spare tire had been put on, and Brother Cyril and I in his new pickup. We were very, very fortunate that everything was in tack and nothing was ruined or lost. The diocesan personnel in Dodoma were very good to us. We decided not to try to get the tiles to Shinyanga in our truck. They gave us a store room to put them in until at some future date we could come and pick them up. You will see how we did it in a future explanation.

Queen of Peace Youth Center

St. Barnabas
June 11, 1991

Dear Dorothy,

Thank you for your two letters which came on the same day, one with the picture and article of Sr. Leonarda.

At first I thought the picture was of mom, but then I saw the nun's garb. As Sister gets older, she is getting to look a lot like mom.

I know you are wondering when I am coming home. It keeps getting later and later as more things come up. There is a "homecoming" at Maryknoll, N.Y. - Sept. 3-5. It is something new for returning missionaries on home leave. I am thinking that I should attend that. I should go to Maryknoll anyways for a visit and to get my will straightened out which is very much out of date having been made in 1957. Also, Fr. Dan Cashman would like me to spend a few days in Ireland. Fr. Dan took my place at Shinyanga Secondary School and will also be home in Ireland on leave. So Now I think I will be arriving in Minneapolis after the visit to Maryknoll.

The hostel is in the final stages. The electricity is being connected by the electric company today. The water will be ready and connected in a few more days. I want to fly to Dar on Saturday of this week to pick up the fridge, stove, etc. which has already arrived coming by air freight from Sweden. Fortunately there is a new 3 ton truck waiting in Dar to be driven to Shinyanga. The truck is a gift to the diocese. I am thinking I could drive the truck and bring the household things in it for the hostel.

I have been working hard to get the hostel ready for the youth directors' seminar to be held July 4-8. I think we will be able to use it for sleeping quarters for our guests. They can have all their meals here at the youth center. We expect 20 to 25 people.

It is 5:45 P.M. now and so I must bring this letter to Brother Cyril at Buhangija since he is leaving tomorrow morning for Nairobi and the U.S. I will ask him to mail this to you when he arrives in the U.S. which will save a couple of day's delivery time.

Greetings to all……
                    With love and prayers,
                    Fr. Marvin

P.S. I guess I forgot your birthday again - Sorry

Footnote:

I want to explain how I got the ceramic tiles to Shinyanga. I discussed with Brother Cyril a way to get them here. He agreed to send his diocesan 1 ton pickup to Dodoma. On my way back from Dar, driving the 3 tonner, I would meet the drivers there, (one of the driver's name was Doto), help them load up the pickup with the tiles and proceed in our two vehicles returning to Shinyanga. I figured out a way to keep the tiles which would be in wooden boxes from being broken by bouncing on the bad roads. We would put two by fours across the top of the boxes and tie them to the sides of the truck. Thus the boxes would not jump around but go up and down with the truck minimizing the jolt.

When I got to Dar, I bought many things I needed for the priests' hostel project, loaded them up in the truck and headed for Dodoma. When I got there, I was happy to see that our two drivers had arrived with the pickup. We loaded up the tiles, tied the boxes down and were ready to go. I told them that I would go ahead of them but would wait for them at the town of Manyoni, a day's journey ahead where we would spend the night. I got to the town of Manyoni about 5:30 PM. I waited and waited but the pickup did not come.

After about an hour, I decided to turn around, go back and see what happened to Doto and his companion. I went back perhaps about 40 miles and found them parked alongside the road. They said they had a flat tire but could not put on the spare because the spare didn't have sufficient air and they had no pump. I asked why they didn't check the spare before they left. They had no answer. I saw an adjacent road leading up to a mission and so decided to go up there to see if I could borrow a pump. I ran across a big truck coming down that road, stopped it and asked the driver if he had a pump. He said no, but he did have a way to put air into our tire with a gadget that fastened on to his engine and acted as a pump. He graciously helped us. We got air into the tire and proceeded on to Manyoni where we spent the night. I stayed at the Catholic Mission and they stayed in a small hotel. The next day we drove all day from early in the morning until evening and made it back to Shinyanga. The road was miserable, but our invention of holding down the boxes in the rear, worked. Only one tile out of a couple of hundred was broken.

Queen of Peace Youth Center

July 18, 1991

Dear Dorothy,

Received your letter written on June 26 and also a couple of others since I have written. Good news - We used the hostel for the first time for the youth directors workshop which was held here from July 4 - 8th. We will use it again next week to house some of the visiting priests coming for the ordinations which will take place in the new cathedral.. There are 3 ordinations this year. The shell is up now for the cathedral. It looks pretty good. There is a lot of work to be done in the interior, but just to get the structure up is very encouraging.

Our bishop, Castor Sekwa, is not even here to participate in all the excitement. He has been in the hospital in Nairobi for some time. The joints in his hips are disintegrating - a rheumatoid condition. The doctors replaced one hip with a plastic socket a couple of weeks ago and will replace the second hip socket on July 31. Bishop Mayalla from the neighboring diocese of Mwanza will come next week to do the ordinations. I talked to our bishop on the phone 2 days ago. He has a good attitude and is determined to recover from all his illnesses.

When I was in Dar es Salaam, I was able to get my plan for home leave lined up and tickets purchased. I have enclosed my schedule. It will be great to see you again.
Love and greetings to you and all,
Fr. Marvin

After the ordination - in front of the partially finished cathedral

Chapter V

Drafted to finish the interior and some exterior design of the Cathedral

Home Leave - 1991

The above is the last saved letter before home leave. I still have the itinerary that I sent to Dorothy with the last letter. I left Tanzania on August 26th, 1991 and returned on Nov. 23rd.   I first flew to Dublin where I was met by Fr. Dan Cashman. He gave me a tour of the country. I left Ireland on Aug. 31 and flew to New York.   I spent about a week at Maryknoll, N.Y. attending the Home-coming with my fellow missionaries also home on leave. From there I went to Minneapolis where I stayed with my sister, Dorothy. I was there until Nov. 20th.

I had quite a bit to do. Before I left, the Bishop asked me to take the cathedral plans with me, find an architect in Minneapolis and ask him to change the sanctuary plan. He was following the advice of Fr. Richard Hochwalt, his vicar general, who said the sanctuary as designed was too small, especially for ordinations and other big events in the cathedral. Also, the African from Nairobi who was in charge of putting the beams up which became the main structural support for the cathedral, came to see me asking if I could get materials in the U.S. for the upper walls. He said the red metal sheeting we have for the walls, if put up, will ruin the looks of the cathedral. I consulted with the Bishop about this and he said that he agrees with this suggestion and asked me to try to get the proper materials. That meant that I would have to send over a container which would involve a tremendous amount of work.

And so, here we go again. Just when I thought I was getting out of the construction business, I was becoming involved again in a huge project - the cathedral. As this story unfolds, you will see what I mean.

One of the first things I did when I got to Minneapolis was to try to find an architect who could modify the sanctuary of the cathedral. In the 1960's, when I was doing promotion work for Maryknoll, I had met a young architect who asked me if there was anything he could do for me. He wanted to design a church that could be built in Africa. I remember very well. - My predecessor, Fr.Dan Ohmann was getting ready to go to Africa on his first missionary assignment. He said he would like the design of a small, round church which could be put up rather simply. My friend produced a very nice design. Actually, Fr. Dan built this church in Africa. It was an out-station church to the central mission of Ndoleleji. I think the name of the outstation was Mhunze. Anyhow, I called up this man. His partner answered the phone and said that my friend had died a few years before. He also said that he knew very little about churches and didn't feel qualified to help me. Somebody - I can't remember who - suggested that I contact Mr. Moudry who was involved in liturgical design. Mr. Moudry used to be Father Moudry. I knew him from my former days working in the Archdiocese of St. Paul and Minneapolis. Moudry was no help either. What to do? It is always best to pray about it and marvelous things happen.

I put the whole project out of my mind for a while. I went to see my dentist, Paul, a good man who always worked on my teeth without charge. Sitting there in the dentist chair, I expressed my frustration at not finding an architect to modify the sanctuary of the cathedral. He said to me, "I know who will do it for you - Jerry Rauenhorst.. He is a graduate from St. Thomas College and is very generous to the Church." And so I said to my dentist. "Give me his telephone number and I will give him a call sometime." Paul said to me, "I want you to call him right away." He went over to the telephone book, looked up his phone number, dialed the number and handed the phone to me. The one who answered was a secretary who said that Mr. Rauenhorst was out of town, but she said that she would get back to me in a few days' time.

About a week later, my sister Dorothy and I were getting ready to make a trip to South Dakota to visit our two aunts, Sr. Leonarda and Sr. Hugonia at Yankton. Before leaving we were preparing a lunch to eat along the way. The phone rang. My sister answered it. The person who called wanted to talk to Father Maryknoll. She handed the phone to me. I said I was not Father Maryknoll, but a member of the Maryknoll society. She said that her boss, Mr. Rauenhorst would be happy to help me and that I should come with the plans to be modified. I told her that I would be gone for a few days but would come in as soon as I got back from my trip.

When Dorothy and I returned from our trip, I looked at the map to determine where Mr. Rauenhorst office was. The secretary had given me the address. I looked at the map and saw only a big blank space where his office was supposed to be (where the freeway 494 and highway 18 came together). And so I called the secretary up. She said that I must have an old map. All these streets are new and now fully developed. I got in my sister's Plymouth and drove to the location which was only about 20 minutes away. I went up to the top floor and asked to see Mr. Rauenhorst. The secretary said that his assistant was assigned to help me. His assistant invited me into his office. We had such a nice conversation. He said he was a graduate of St. John's in Collegeville. I found out that his boss, Jerry Rauenhorst, was a student at St. Thomas College the same time that I was there. His partner took me out on the penthouse roof and showed me some of the big buildings nearby. I pointed to one which I especially admired. He said that he had designed that building. This was a most pleasant experience. I felt that the grace of God was working overtime. He said when the project was finished that I would receive a call.

Shortly after that I had to see my dentist friend, Paul, again. I thanked him for introducing me to his good friend. Paul said to me, "I don't know Jerry. In fact, I have never met him. I just knew that he would help you." About a week later I got the call and went down to pick up the finished plans. This time another architect called me into his cubicle. He is the one who did the actual work. It was a very nice job. I knew the Bishop would be pleased with the new design for the sanctuary. He also penciled in where the pews should go. This man said he was a graduate from the University of Minnesota. I don't recall his name.

It was shortly after this experience that I was visiting my twin sister, Marlys, on Margaret street in St. Paul. She and her husband, Floyd, had just had the siding on their house redone with aluminum siding. As soon as I saw it, I said - "That's the answer. Now I know how to finish the upper walls of the Cathedral - with white aluminum siding." Aluminum does not rust. It will last for ages. Now I knew what I had to do. I had to buy a construction board which would be covered by the siding and for the inside of the upper wall - 4 by 8 wood paneling. I will get together a container and have it sent out by Brother Regis in New Holstein Wisconsin. By the grace of God, things were beginning to fall into place.

During home leave I showed a video of my work at my home parish, St. Helena's in South Minneapolis. In the picture, Sr. Joan, the parish worker, is asking me some questions about my work. My sister, Dorothy is looking on. My home leave was quite productive. I was able to get the materials I would need for the Cathedral project and also return with the new plan for the cathedral sanctuary. The following letter was written shortly after my return to Tanzania.

Return to Tanzania from Home Leave

Maryknoll Fathers
Dar es Salaam
Tanzania

Tuesday, Nov. 19, 1991

Dear Dorothy,

Greetings from Dar es Salaam. It is good to have both feet on the ground. Things worked out real well on the way. When I arrived at the airport in Amsterdam on Friday morning, I went right to the hotel desk. The girl there said there was no problem and gave me a voucher for the Hilton Hotel which is less than a half mile from the airport. A small courtesy bus takes you there free of charge. Everything at the hotel was paid for by the airlines. I had a nice room and 3 meals - supper, breakfast and lunch the next day.

The airplane from Mpls to Amsterdam was only about half filled. However, the flight from Amsterdam to Dar es Salaam was fully booked - not an empty seat. I sat next to an Americana black who works for the World Bank in Dar. His name is Darius Mans. Darius was a very friendly, pleasant chap. It is a long flight from Amsterdam to Dar - 8 1/2 hours nonstop. The plane left at mid- night and arrived at 8:30 A.M. or 10:30 A.M .local time. I had no trouble with customs. The fellow just asked me what I was building with the tools. Fr Howie O'Brien was there to meet me, which really made me glad - no problem at all getting the baggage out to the house. He told me right away that the shipping documents for the container had already arrived so that problem was solved too.

On Monday Fr. John Lange came in from Kibaha. I was able to give him all the news and greetings from so many who asked to be remembered. Today is Tuesday. This morning we made photo copies of all the container papers so that is done too. I haven't decided which day I will leave for the up-country. Thomas Shadtweiler, the German fellow who is the agricultural worker in Shinyanga, is waiting for his new wife to come from Germany. He would like to fly, but if he can't get a plane, there is a possibility of him driving a new vehicle just arrived for Shinyanga and then we could go together. So I am waiting a couple of days to see who that turns out.

The weather is hot and humid like it always is this time of year (90) in Dar es Salaam. They had some rain over a week ago, but now everything is dry. I hear it is the same in Shinyanga which should make it easy driving. My body clock is not in sync yet with the local time. I am awake at night and sleep in the day time. It will take about a week to get straightened out..

Greetings to all....
Love and prayers,
Fr. Marvin

Queen of Peace Youth Center
Shinyanga
Tanzania

December 8, 1991

Dear Dorothy,

You get two Christmas letters this year. This personal one and the more general one for everybody. I have been back at the youth center over two weeks and this is my first letter to you. It was good talking to you on the phone. I am happy to hear you got some information on how Deb is doing, although I think she should contact you. Perhaps she will in time.

I have done quite a lot since coming back. I have all the accounts straightened out now. I have pruned all the trees which grew into a jungle while I was gone. I did a lot of repairs. It's amazing how many things got broken in a few months' time. I hired 7 workers again. Five of them have started putting in the rough floor at the diocesan office block conference center. One is a carpenter who has started making the beds. He has 4 beds made now.

The Bishop has an ordination to the diaconate in the cathedral on December 27 and wants to use the new priests' hostel for guests. By that time we should have about 15 beds made. The new roof on the cathedral was leaking. I helped sealing the leaks with caulking material which works wonders.

We have a seminar here at the center this week for about 15 youth. Brother Kevin is helping with that. There has been some rain but not enough for planting. Our place is very green, however. In fact, it looks lovely.

May the peace and happiness of Christmas be yours today and every day throughout the coming New Year.

Love and prayers,
Fr. Marvin

Ordination to the Diaconate - Dec. 27, 1991

The first picture: Some of the Irish priests (SMA) sitting next to the Bishop on his right. On the left of the Bishop is African Father Zachary Buluba, the senior African priest in the diocese. The Bishop was still in good health when this picture was taken. In the above picture, the bell tower is in the background (without the bells). The white haired priest is Fr. Dan Cashman who took my place in 1988 at Shinyanga Secondary School. I am in both pictures if you look closely.

319

"In His body lives the fullness of Divinity, and in Him you too find your own fulfillment, in the one who is the head of every Sovereignty & Power"
(Col: 2.9-10)

DEC. 8, 1991

QUEEN of PEACE
YOUTH CENTER

Dear friends,

It is that beautiful time of year again when we take time out to say hello to friends. Thank God for Christmas. A year ago the two youth in the picture above made the plywood cutouts of the crib scene which we displayed outside in the space in front of the youth center auditorium. It was interesting watching the reactions of the passersby. Some hardly noticed. Others stopped and stared. Some knelt right down on the side of the road to pray. . Each of us reacts in his own way depending upon one's faith. How many today believe the statement above from Colossians? If everyone sought his or her fulfillment in that little baby, we would have quite a different world.

This past year has been a year of growth here at the youth center both physically and spiritually. From the size of the trees and shrubs, one would think that the center has been around a lot longer than the two and a half years it has been open. By good fortune it was built on 5 feet of rich black topsoil, the best land I have seen in Tanzania. In other ways the center has been very fruitful. Hundreds of youth come to this place for various activities, including sports, domestic science courses, use of the library, retreats, etc.

God bless you this Christmas season. May our Blessed Mother protect you in the New Year just as she did her child Jesus.

Christmas love and peace,
Fr. Marvin

Dar es Salaam

Jan. 25, 1992

Dear Dorothy,

Perhaps you have been trying to call me. Both Brother Kevin and I were at the regional meeting, Jan. 5-10 in Musoma. Now I am in Dar es Salaam having flown here on Jan. 17 on the Mwadui Diamonds Mines plane. I came here to get paints and other building supplies, foam mattresses etc. which I will bring back to Shinyanga in the new high school 3 ton truck. I also came to check on the container. It has been a successful trip. The container is not only in, it is all cleared through customs and is now sitting in the yard of the transporter who will transport it to Shinyanga in about 2 weeks' time. I was present when the customs people opened the container. Everything looked all right.

Also, I was able to buy many of the other needed things while here. Fr. John Lange paid for 30 foam rubber mattresses and 35 foam chair sets which was certainly kind of him. He was here overnight. We celebrated his 61st birthday. Brother John Wohead came with me to Dar and will drive back with me in the truck. We have everything loaded and expect on leave tomorrow (Sunday) after mass. The first part of this trip is easy, 300 miles to Dodoma on a tarmac road.

Enclosed are 4 checks totaling $115. Also, I wrote a check for $2,300 which will pay for most of the transport of the container. The remaining $700 will not be paid until the container arrives. It is a 600 mile trip. I hope this gets to you a little faster since it is being mailed here in Dar.

Take care, love and prayers.

Fr. Marvin

Footnote:

Bishop Castor had recovered from his hip surgery. His bigger health problems lay ahead when he would come down with a brain tumor. The container with all the building materials I needed to complete the diocesan office block and conference room and also the cathedral had arrived in Dar. A Goan whose name was Raul, who ran a transport business, was going to bring the container on its 600 mile journey. I had agreed to pay him in dollars with a check being sent to an address in Canada. If I had paid him in Tanzanian Shillings, he would not have been able to convert these into dollars. Tanzanian shillings were worthless on the international market. Poor countries needed "foreign exchange" which consisted of dollars, Deutsch marks, British pounds, or Japanese yen, in order to buy things outside their own countries. That is why I gave Raul a dollar check and had it sent it to an address in Canada so he could use this money to buy things outside the country of Tanzania.

Queen of Peace Youth Center

Feb. 24, 1992

Dear Dorothy,

The good news is that the container has arrived. It came on Feb. 20, Thursday, about noon. The driver said he had left on the previous Saturday which meant that his safari took 5 1/2 days. He said he went slowly to prevent breakages on the very bad roads. I have unpacked many of the things and so far I have found nothing broken and everything just as we packed it. I already have mom's microwave set up and am now using it daily to heat up my cup of coffee etc. I have also used the broom type vacuum cleaner which makes rug cleaning very easy. Speaking of rugs - the one you made with the deer image is now in my room. It is soft and fluffy and really looks nice. And of course, with the building materials, we can now finish the diocesan office block and the cathedral. I have already started on the terrazzo floor. I found a good man who is reasonable and knows what he is doing. He is training my workers which will keep the cost down.

Perhaps we will be able to start the upper walls of the cathedral in about a week's time. And so everything is turning out nicely. I know there were a lot of prayers said by you and Sister Leonarda for which I am grateful. Our Bishop has been in Nairobi for a checkup for the past 3 weeks. I am sure he will be surprised at the progress made in his absence.

Lent is coming up soon. May it be a holy one.
Love and prayers,
Fr. Marvin

Footnote:

There are several things which need to be explained in the above letter. My mother had died in 1986. My siblings wanted me to take something of her belongings in memory of her. I took the microwave. It was not until 1992 that I found a use for it - sending it to Tanzania in the container. I had to send a transformer along with it since in Tanzania we have the 240 Volt system and not 110-20 in the U.S. But it worked just fine with the transformer.

As regards the terrazzo floor in the cathedral - this was a big operation. Terrazzo is a mixture of white cement and fine pebbles of various colors depending on the color you want the finished product to look like. Plastic strips are laid out on the floor in squares or various designs. The cement mixture is poured into these sections. When it is hard, a machine with grinding stones is used to make the surface smooth. The finished product is very nice. It looks almost like marble. The man I hired started out very well.

He finished doing the sacristy and the sanctuary. I would check on him every day to make sure he was laying out the strips in the proper design and mixing the cement and pebbles properly etc. Then he got into the main body of the church, I saw he was not doing it right. I had to rearrange the strips correctly. I knew he was drinking heavily. Then one day he had the workers pour the cement mixture over a large area without preparing the sub - concrete floor area properly. This had to be very clean. I asked him why he was doing this. He gave me some excuse that he knew what he was doing. Anyhow, a couple of days later, he took off. He just disappeared. Someone said he went home to Bukoba, a city on the western side of Lake Victoria. I was exasperated. I had my workers chop out what had been done wrong. It took a whole month. I knew that if we didn't do this, eventually the floor would come loose. Fortunately my workers now knew how to do the job and we finally got it done.

The bishop, Caster Sekwa, was in Nairobi for three weeks having a checkup. He was diagnosed with a brain tumor. His days were numbered as you will see in future letters. Fortunately he lived long enough to see the Cathedral finished.

Queen of Peace Youth Center

March 1, 1992

Dear Bob and Grace,

> *I am happy to tell you that the container arrived on Feb. 20. I want to thank you for helping me with the transport of materials from Minneapolis to New Holstein, Wisconsin so that they could be shipped overseas in the container. Thanks too to your son, Freddie for the use of his truck.*
>
> *We had no crane to offload the container after it had been emptied, so the driver hitched up a chain, fastened it around a tree and around the container and pulled it off. It went bump-bump, but landed O.K.*
>
> *It was all a lot of work but very worthwhile. We can now finish the work on the diocesan hostel and cathedral, plus having a lot of nice things. Thanks again for your help.... God bless you...*
>
>
>
> *Love and prayers,*
> *Fr. Marvin*
>
>

Footnote:

Grace and Bob Sharpe were good friends and came to my rescue when I had no truck to transport things from Mpls. to New Holstein, Wisconsin. Bob went with me on the trip.

Queen of Peace Youth Center
P.O. Box 47, Shinyanga
Tanzania

April 1, 1992

Dear Dorothy,

Thanks very much for your letter of March 2 with all the good news. I will get a note off to Emma Kleve right away for her very generous gift. Yes, we really are enjoying all the things from the container. I use the microwave every day. It is especially nice for heating up things and making my cup of coffee. I use the bicycle every day going back and forth to the building project on the Bishops compound which saves me a lot of steps and time. It is a little over 100 yards away.

The Cathedral is coming along nicely. The internal work is my responsibility. The terrazzo floor is finished in the sacristy and about 3/4 finished in the sanctuary. After another week of grinding and polishing, that will be done too. The Bishop wants to use the cathedral for the Good Friday and Easter celebrations. The upper side walls of the cathedral are slow going because all the studs have to be bolted in, but that is beginning to move too. I have two excellent carpenters doing the work. At the priest's hostel, we have begun the roof rafters for the office block. The first couple of rafters will be erected today.

Brother Kevin leaves for home leave this Friday, April 3. I think he did very well teaching religion in the secondary schools and deserves a good rest. He said he will be with his mom for Easter. I think she is in her 70's. I will have extra work to do with Kevin gone, but there are just so many hours in a day. Some things will have to be left undone. I am not teaching anymore in the secondary schools. All this construction is something I never dreamed I would be doing.

I offered mass for you the other day for your birthday. This year I did not forget your birthday although I didn't get a card out to you. I hope this gets to you by Easter. Greetings to Deb and Marg and all. A very happy, blessed and joy filled Easter.

Much love and prayers,

Fr. Marvin

Queen of Peace Youth Center

May 3, 1992

Dear friends,

Greetings - Easter is now history and it is already May. Over 5 months have passed since I returned from home leave in the U.S. The container which took a lot of my time preparing - which was filled with building materials, sewing materials and all kinds of other things including a bicycle which was a gift from a friend, Louise Sharpe, arrived here in late February. With the help of these materials, I have been able to move along the building projects - the supervision of which was given to me by Bishop Sekwa. The 22 bedroom hostel which is primarily for the African priests, was 90% finished before I went home on leave. The administration part which will be the new offices of the Bishop and his staff, and the conference room, was started in early December. This week the corrugated iron sheets will be put on the roof. There is a meeting planned for all the priests of the diocese in Sept. I hope to have everything finished by then.

Finishing the cathedral is more complicated and will take longer. We built a huge portable scaffold to help with the construction of the side upper walls. When I say portable I mean that a dozen men can lift it and move it along as needed. The terrazzo floor is now finished in the sacristy and sanctuary. We have just started in the main body of the church. The target date for the completion of the cathedral is Christmas of this year.

Twenty years ago - if someone had told me I would be doing this kind of construction, I would not have believed it. I remember our pastor, Monsignor Rowan, back around 1938-39, walking along the roof structure of the edifice which was to be St. Helena's church in Minneapolis. I guess I am about as old now as he was then. He seemed undaunted by any problems.

The youth work continues to go well here at Queen of Peace Youth Center. Over 100 students attended the 4 day retreat during Holy Week ending on Easter Sunday. The theme of the retreat was "It is in Christ that we find true freedom and it is in him that we become the new creation." The response was excellent which is very encouraging.

We had a rather poor rainy season, but now it is raining very heavily - about 7 inches the past 10 days. Most of the corn was lost but with these rains there will be plenty of sweet potatoes. I am not much of a writer these days. When evening comes I look forward to crawling into bed. But I want you to know how much I appreciate your prayers and help. I am saying many masses and prayers for you good people...

Blessings in the Lord,
Fr. Marvin.

Bishop Sekwa with statue donated by Ireland

Congratulating the young ladies who just finished the sewing course

Queen of Peace Youth Center

Sunday, August 9, 1992

Dear Dorothy,

I just reread your letter of July 1 in which you mentioned that Mary Lou Heskett might call. She did and said she couldn't believe how easy it was and how the connection was so clear. I asked her to call you right away. I have written so few letters these past months, but at least through the telephone you know that everything is O.K. here.

Brother Kevin has been back since July 12, but he had to be off again to attend the Maryknoll board meeting in Musoma. He has been gone one week but I expect him back tomorrow.

The youth center continues to be in great demand from many sources. Fr. Peter Le Jacq, who is also a doctor, came with 3 people and stayed overnight. He went down to Tabora, about 120 miles from here, to give an AIDS conference to the diocese of Tabora. Two people with him, a man and a woman, have AIDS and help Peter with his talks. The young man is pretty far advanced and probably won't live another year, but he wants to do what he can to help others not to contact this terrible disease.

This past week about 15 doctors from various parts of Tanzania held their meeting here for 3 days. They used our auditorium which is ideal for meetings. They furnished their own food and lodging. I asked the doctor who organized the meeting why he wanted to use the youth center, and he said - it is quiet here and the atmosphere is very nice. Our trees and shrubs are big now and even the patio outside the meeting room is well sheltered with trees which provide shade for sitting outside during the break time. We put tables and chairs out there for that purpose.

The construction of the priests' hostel-office block, conference center is going along nicely. There were enough ceramic (Italian) tiles left to do the conference room, the bishop's new office and 2 other rooms. A touch of elegance, I would say.

The cathedral is moving along too, although we have a problem with part of the terrazzo. About one third of the main body of the church has to be chipped out and done over. The man I had hired to supervise the work was not paying his skilled workers so they quit on him. He hired cheap unskilled labor in their place and they botched the job. The man himself took off without telling me, evidently aware that I would discover the mistake and make him do it over again at quite an expense to him. Anyhow, I am using all my own workers now I have a fellow, Luhende, who learned the terrazzo work by helping the man who took off, and so he is now quite qualified.

Tuesday morning, Aug II

As you can see I didn't finish this letter on Sunday. Since then Brother Kevin is back. Also, your letter of July 22 came. I was curious about Steve coming back to live at your house. If you are happy about it, that's what matters, but I still think he should have his own place when he gets more financially settled. But it is your decision to make.

Fr. Dan Omann brought Brother Kevin back from Musoma and stayed overnight. I prepared a fillet mignon supper which he said was better than he had in the U.S. We have excellent equipment here. I used one of the new, no stick, teflon frying pans which came in the container. So many things from the container are helping us now.

Yesterday, my 2 carpenters finished putting wood paneling in the new office for the bishop at the office-block-conference center. The back wall behind his desk will be the only wall paneled. We have also started to panel the back wall of the conference room which will really set it off.

The cloth materials which came from all your lady friends are a tremendous help, not only for the sewing class (the present class has 20 including 2 boys, the biggest group so far), but also for making curtains for the new conference center. We also covered over 40 chair cushions. The investment of time and money to prepare all the things for the container shipment is now worth 10 times what we put into it.

Best wishes to all. Tell Margaret I appreciate her letter. I am happy that she quit the job at Target. It is better to be a little poorer than to have to work that hard.

Love and prayers,

Fr. Marvin

Footnote:

The meeting with Fr. Peter Le Jacq was very revealing. The young man with AIDS who came with him, gave us a very honest run down of his lifestyle. He said he had a different woman for sex almost every night. The theory is that the more sex partners a person has, the possibility of getting AIDS goes up geometrically. One who does this is bound to have a partner who has AIDS. The question is -

why is there so much promiscuity? We all know, of course, that the sexual revolution has brought about a huge change in attitudes on the morality of sex. Sexual license is even promoted. The availability of indecent movies and videos is everywhere. In my work as teacher and youth director, I teach about the importance of abstinence - of living in union with Jesus Christ, not only to prevent getting AIDS, but even more importantly, to live the life of grace leading to the salvation of one's soul. We had the Young Christian Students organization which is quite successful in promoting Catholic principles regarding sex and morality. I considered my teaching in the high schools and the retreat work at the youth center as the most important of all my work. I teach the students that if they keep the 10 commandments, the AIDS pandemic in a few years will disappear.

Nairobi

Sept. 17, 1992

Dear Bob and Grace,

Greetings from Nairobi, I didn't expect to be up here at our society house this time of year, but after a bout with malaria, I took the good advice of taking a few days off. Nairobi is 600 miles from Shinyanga, but I came up the easy way. I drove to Mwanza - a rugged trip of 100 miles, left my pick up there and flew the rest of the way in a 6 seater Cessna belonging to the African Inland Church, a Protestant organization offering services to medical and missionary people. We made one stop on the way up, coming down on a tiny air

---

strip in the bush, a place called Shirati, to leave off some medicines at the Mennonite hospital there. All the children came running to the plane as we taxied to a stop - a big event in their lives. The pilot checked to make sure all the cows were off the runway and we were off again. I have been in Nairobi for about 10 days. Tomorrow I will return the same way I came.

Just about a year has passed since we were making our trips to New Holstein, Wisconsin. The blandex, 4 by 8 sheets now cover the ceiling in the 7 room office block-conference center. The construction board covers the upper outer walls of the cathedral, etc. etc. Without all the good things that came in the container, the job could not have been done. Thanks to you and all the help you gave me. When I left Shinyanga, the biggest sewing class we ever had with 20 participants was going on. Even the knitting needles were being used.

Thanks for your letter of June 23 and the lovely pictures of your 50th. Looking at the picture, one would think you were never sick a day in your life - quite contrary to the reality. You mentioned the cool weather. I understand the rest of the summer was cool also. The weather patterns everywhere seem to be following extremes of hot-cold; dry-wet, etc. In the country south of us, Zimbabwe, they are experiencing the worst drought of the century. I heard that the city of Bulmeyo, which has over a million people, will run out of water in a couple of week's time.

In Tanzania food supplies are short, especially maize. The water behind the dam which furnishes the electric power for the entire country is getting low. Electricity is now being rationed - one day off, one day on. We are hoping for early rains. Some years there are good rains in October which would be a Godsend this year. Hope this finds you both fully recovered.

Love and prayers,
Fr. Marv

P.S. Special greetings to Freddie - also please tell Louise that I use the bicycle she gave me almost every day going between the youth center and the diocesan construction site. It saves a lot of time.

Footnote:

I also, while in Nairobi, wrote a letter to my sister, Dorothy. Rather than repeating what I wrote above, I will add a few things here which were not in the above letter.

Nairobi

Sept. 14, 1992

Dear Dorothy,

A week has gone by (since arriving in Nairobi) . I have had lots of rest, did some shopping and also visited a skin specialist, Dr. Kahn, a woman doctor who treats many of our people. I had a small growth behind my left ear which was caused by too much exposure to the sun. These growths turn into skin cancer if left untreated. The treatment is quite simple. They spray on some liquid nitrogen, which burns out the core of the growth. It blisters, scabs over, and heals in about 2 weeks. The doctor advised me to wear a wide brimmed hat and use a good sun- tan lotion on the troubled areas.

Enclosed is a $3 check from Joe Lowery for my account. I met Joe in 1951 at Glen Ellyn. He was a seminarian at St. Procopius seminary, a few miles from our seminary. Joe did not go on to the priesthood. Somehow he found out where I am and now writes to me occasionally.

I will be flying out of here on Friday, Sept. 18.
With love and prayers,
Fr. Marvin

P.S. Fr. John Lange is due here the first week in October to become the house manager of our Nairobi house.

STAGE II
applying the construction boa to the studs

Building the upper walls of the Cathedral

STAGE I
fastening the wooden studs to the steel frame

Stage III - applying the aluminum siding over the construction board

Queen of Peace Youth Center

Oct. 25, 1992

Dear Dorothy,

    Received your letter of Sept. 30 a few days ago. Many thanks - also for the nice pictures. I didn't recognize

Catherine Longen right away. She has filled out a little but looks good. It is amazing how Sr. Hugonia improves when you come. I think someone new in her life is better than medicine.

This is my first letter since coming back from Nairobi. Things are going good now with the construction as you can see from the enclosed pictures. I wish it all could go a bit faster, but the big thing is that everything is done right. The Bishop wants the conference center-hostel ready for the African priests' retreat beginning Nov. 15. I think we will make it. The conference room looks great with the front and back walls paneled. The front wall has a black board surrounded by paneling. The shrine to our Blessed Mother turned out lovely and is the focal point of the patio.

There are so many youth activities these days both in the schools and here at the center. I am getting a little nap every day, but it is not so easy with all the activities. I plan to go to Nairobi for a vacation in December. I haven't heard from Rita and Bob, whether or not they are coming out.

The month of October brings back a lot of memories from last year - the trips to Wisconsin, to South Dakota, and the big snow storm. A lot has been accomplished this past year. I think the work has gone slow, but when I think of all the changes here since last December, it really hasn't.

We had our first big rain - over an inch. I hope it continues. The grass here is turning green.

> *My love and prayers,*
> *Fr. Marvin*

Footnote:

Catherine Longen was my first cousin. Rita was my sister, two years younger than I. She and her husband, Bob, were contemplating a trip to Africa which never materialized. October of 1991, the year before while I was home, was a very exciting one. I had gotten the new plans for the Cathedral from Jerry Rauendhorst. Also my sister Dorothy and I had gone to South Dakota. First we went to visit my favorite cousin, Joe Deutsch and his wife Edythe who lived in Eden. S. Dakota. While there we had watched on TV The Minnesota Twins played the Atlanta Braves in the World Series. It went to 7 games. The game was saved by Kirby Puckett who made a leaping catch in left field and so the Twins won. It started to rain-snow while we were there, but we still drove South to Yankton to see my two aunts, Sr. Leonarda and Sr. Hugonia..

We were there a couple of days and were hesitant in leaving in Dorothy's small car, a 1984 Plymouth Horizon, because of the snow storm which was getting worse and worse. We decided to try to make the 300 miles journey. As we were going along highway 29 heading towards Sioux Falls, South Dakota, we saw many cars in the ditch. The little Horizon which had front wheel drive was doing O.K. It was a terrible day for driving. Big semis were going by us splashing snow and ice. We moved on taking highway 60 from Worthington to St. Paul. We got almost to Shakopee which was only about 30 miles from our destination, when the car began to stall. I pulled off on the exit trying to make it to a filling station, I didn't make it. The car stopped. It was about 4:30 P.M. and soon it would be dark. What to do? I said to Dorothy, "Let's say a Hail Mary". We did that. I got out of the car, opened the hood and looked at the engine, not sure what I was looking for. I noticed a big chunk of ice had formed on the fuel filter. I knocked the chunk of ice off, closed the hood and went back into the car to see if it would start.   After about a minute of grinding away, it started and then after another minute began to purr along normally. That was it. The fuel line had become frozen. We were able to make it the rest of the way. There were cars off the road. It was a miserable evening.

When we got to Dorothy's house in South Minneapolis, the snow was at least a foot deep. I opened the garage door and pulled the car into the garage. We went into the house with our luggage. We couldn't believe it. There were beer cans strewn here and there. Debbie, Dorothy's adopted daughter, was nowhere to be seen. I checked to see if there was any altar wine left because I wanted to say mass the next morning in the house. The wine bottle was empty. I said to Dorothy - "I am going to the liquor store (about a mile away) to get some wine. Even though the snow was deep, the little car was able to make it there and back. I got the wine. Dorothy was in a state of shock. We knew that Steve, Debbie's boyfriend was emotionally unstable, but we did not expect this, that they would take off together.

The next day, because of the wind, a big drift had formed in front of the garage door. I couldn't get the door open until I could shovel away the drift. But I was not in a hurry to go any place. I was very thankful to God that we had made it home in one piece. We were fortunate indeed. I don't think it is appropriate to tell the story about Steve and Debbie here. The story does not have a happy ending.

Queen of peace Youth Center

St. Nicolas
December 6, 1992

Dear Dorothy,

I just received your letter of Nov. 19th a couple of days ago. Many thanks. The African priests' retreat is being held in the new hostel December 14-18. It had to be postponed in November because things were not quite ready. The water supply from the town is hopeless these days which means that the water has to be carried in buckets from our rain water reserve tanks. You can imagine carrying water to flush a dozen toilets for over 20 people. Anyhow I am building a super duper 5 room outdoor toilet which takes no water at all. It will be ready by the retreat.

The last couple of days I have been opening the last of the boxes from the container, the ones with the pots and pans and other things for the kitchen at the priests' hostel which is really shaping up nicely. We will finish all the cupboards and the hutch this week, so I think all will be ready for the retreat. Brother Kevin will be supervising the cooking just during the retreat. He has put together a pretty good staff. The only problem I see is the water. The electricity has been regularized since there has been enough rain at the dam site to bring up the water level a little. The rains, however, are very slow in coming. Two weeks ago we had a week of rain totaling 6 inches which was terrific. But suddenly it stopped. Today there was a return of a heavy cloud formation, so perhaps this week we will get some rain.

This German fellow, Matthias Braun, who comes here to play tennis on Sunday afternoons with Brother Cyril and I, is going to Nairobi again so I am asking him to mail this letter there hoping you will get it sooner. I will be heading for Nairobi myself about December 18th or 19th and spend Christmas there since the schools will be closed giving me a break.

A lovely and Merry Christmas to you an all....
Love and Prayers,
Fr. Marvin

Queen of Peace Youth Center

Christmas day 1992

Dear Dorothy,
This is Christmas day afternoon. The excitement of the feast day has subsided. And in the quiet and restful atmosphere of my office here at the youth center, I am free to write a few lines to wish you a belated Merry Christmas and all the best in the New Year.

This past year has been a challenging time for me with long hours of work. I think you know that some time ago, our Bishop Caster Sequa placed a big responsibility on me besides my youth work, to build a 23 bedroom hostel which included the new diocesan building headquarters which I had to design plus doing the finishing work on the cathedral. The diocesan offices and conference room are now complete. It was used for the first time for the African priests' retreat Dec. 14-18. My co-worker here at the youth center, Brother Kevin Dargan, a first class chef, supervised the setting up of the kitchen and dining hall as well as all the meals. The youth center now has very good facilities, 2 fridges, a deep freeze, and two electric stoves imported from Sweden. Some of the dishes, pots and pans, mugs, etc. came from our home parish of St. Helena's in Minneapolis. I am sure you remember, when home on leave in 1991 we went to their rummage sale in Rowan Hall and we got a lot of nice things very cheaply which are great to have out here.

The Cathedral, named "Mama wenye Huruma" (Mother of Mercy), was used this morning for the Christmas celebration and 10:30 mass presided over by Bishop Sequa. There were about 2000 people present. It was a great joy for the Bishop, probably the greatest event of his life, fulfilling his dreams of a new cathedral and knowing that with his illness he may not live much longer. I reminded him that St. Peter's in Rome took 175 years to complete so we are not doing too badly. The blessing and official opening is scheduled for May at which time all the Bishops of Tanzania will be invited to attend. I will be happy when all the work is finished so I can get back full time to my youth work.

The rains, which were late this year, have finally come in abundance. Since mid-November we had 11 inches. Africa, which is famine prone, always has us worried. There are some areas in the diocese where the Church is feeding the people since last year was a poor year for the crops and they have no reserve. We hope and pray that the rains will continue and next March - April will see a good harvest.

Today, Christmas day, I said an early mass at the youth center and also later celebrated with the Bishop at the Cathedral. I remembered all of my friends and benefactors in thanksgiving for all the blessings of this past year. In these troubled times in which so much of the world is still in darkness, I pray that all will discover the message of Isaiah, which is in the first reading of the midnight mass:

A child is born to us, a son is given to us...they will call him wonder-counselor, God hero, Father forever, Prince of Peace.

Much love and a Blessed New Year,
Fr. Marvin

Queen of Peace Youth Center

Sunday, Jan. 24, 1993

Dear Dorothy,

Thank you for your letter of Dec. 30 with dividend statement for income tax and also a list of donations and donors. I didn't get to Nairobi as planned. There were problems there because of the first free elections in 26 years (fear of tension and violence) and so I didn't go. Now I plan to go up to Nairobi around Feb. 5 and stay two weeks. A number of the priests who belong to "Yesu Caritas", (a spiritual organization) are making a retreat at the Jesuit retreat center outside Nairobi which I feel is very important to make since I have not made an extended retreat for a long time.

The past two weeks, the Apostolic delegate, Archbishop Augustino Marchetto, has been visiting the diocese. He is a very social person, easy to talk to and also did a lot more than just visit. He visited many parishes with our Bishop and helped with confirmations. Because of all the illnesses that our Bishop has had, he got behind in the confirmations. Now he is all caught up. This morning 500 youth were confirmed at the new cathedral across the way.
We had the delegate here for a meeting with the sisters of the diocese (about 40) after which we served lunch to everyone. It was a good opportunity for him to not only meet the sisters but also to see the youth center.

This evening there is a farewell supper for the delegate at Buhangija parish about 3 miles from here to which we are all invited. Two of the young Irish priests from the SMA Fathers are staying with us. They will attend the supper, stay overnight in our guest house and leave for their parish in the morning. Both like to play tennis so we had a good game about an hour ago. The delegate will return to Dar es Salaam tomorrow via the Mwadui Diamond Mine's plane.

Last Friday was a big day for the clergy. The delegate blessed the new priests' conference center (which I have been working on for over 2 years). A concelebrated mass was held in the cathedral, also which was possible only because of months of work there. I am happy that the conference center is finished. The bishop will be moving in soon to his new office. I still have a water tank to build there, but that should not be too difficult.

We have had 4 inches of rain so far this month of January which is not bad. There is a sense of hope among the people that this year will see a good harvest...

With love and prayers,

Fr. Marvin

347

The 23 bedroom priests' hostel and conference center - finished in time for the African priests' retreat - Dec. 1992

The conference room and Bishop's offices (these 2 pictures are photocopies. I do not have the original pictures)

The Apostolic delegate, Archbishop Augustino Marcheetto and I. - The Archbishop was making a visitation in January 1993 and blessed the new conference center named after Pope John Paul II.

Footnote:

The Problem with the pews for the cathedral:

Another headache connected with building: It was also my responsibility to design and build the pews for the cathedral - no small task. I elicited the help of Joseph Ebricht, a half cast (his father was a German doctor and his mother African). Joseph had the biggest carpenter shop in town with the latest machinery for cutting, planing etc. imported from Italy. Also he was a fine Catholic. We worked on a design for the pews and he suggested that I order the wood from an Indian Singh who had a factory in Tabora about 120 miles South of Shinyanga, where he cut the wood from logs harvested someplace south of there. He said the Singh would deliver the wood in 3 trips, but he insisted on being paid $3000 in advance. I told Joseph that I don't operate that way. When he brings the wood he gets his money. Joseph insisted that I pay ahead and said that I could trust this man. Against my better judgment I gave him a check for $3000. I received only one shipment. The rest never came. I even made a trip to Tabora to try to get the $2000 he owed me back. The Singh said the money was gone and his equipment had broken down. He was building a house for his son who was about to be married. I ended up buying the wood locally. I didn't take Singh to court because it would have tied me up for weeks fighting the case. My time was worth more than the money. I sent Singh a letter telling him he wouldn't get away with what he was doing, that there was a supreme judge he would have to meet one day. I told Bishop Sekwa and he agreed with my decision.

Nairobi

Feb. 17, 1993

Dear Dorothy,

Greetings from Nairobi, I had a wonderful retreat at the Jesuit retreat house on the edge of town in a countrified area - marvelous grounds with lots of trees and vegetation.

There were about 10 in our group - also about 15 others - priests and sisters making private directed retreats.

I got a blood test and a physical while here.: blood count normal, sugar normal, no malaria or intestinal parasites - blood pressure 120/80. The only thing a little high was the cholesterol, but for me that is the usual thing. To tell you the truth, I was surprised that I am in such good shape. Even the liver function test was normal - something which I had trouble with for many years in the past.

I have been doing some shopping while here - a few gallons. of paint, a water pump, jalousie window frames etc. Also I found a nice large tabernacle at the Consolata procure which is just right for the cathedral. The Consolatas have a big store of religious goods all imported from Italy which is a tremendous service to the Church.

Fathers Don Sybertz, Ernie Brunelle and I will be heading back to Tanzania tomorrow. We will take it a little slower going back. Coming up we made it in 2 days, but will take 3 going back. While here I had a tape cassette player installed in my pickup. Nice to play music on these long trips. Also, I have the scripture rosary on tape which makes it very easy to say the rosary while traveling.

Enclosed are a couple of pictures I just had developed. Greetings to Deb, Marg and all...
Love and prayers,
Fr. Marvin

351

Queen of Peace Youth Center

Monday, March 15, 1993

Dear Dorothy,

I have your letters of Feb. 10 and 23. Many thanks. That sure was a big gift from the Kleves. I will write to them. I have a plan for this money and want to use it to help worthy youth to advance their education. I will also write to Alice and Frank Mance to congratulate them on their anniversary. I am sorry to hear that Ralph Douglas is in the hospital. It is amazing that he has been able to carry on as long as he has. He has been on dialysis for such a long time.

Over the weekend we had a vocation awareness workshop here for about 30 form 5 boys (like first year college in the U.S.). Three order priests were here - a Jesuit, a White Father, and a Rosminian. They came from a long ways off - Dar es Salaam, Tanga, and Mwanza. It is good to see the interest, and with the good youth center facilities here, these days are not hard to put on.

The rains have continued regularly this year. Many people are already harvesting. So this is real good news - no famine this year. Lent is going by so fast. I had better get this in the mail to wish you a most blessed and happy Easter.

Love and Prayers,
Fr. Marvin

Queen of Peace Youth Center

May 1, 1993

Dear Dorothy,

Seems like at least a month since I have written. It is good that you can call now and then so we can keep up to date. I sent a card to Lorraine Douglas and also said quite a few masses for Ralph. He had a long ordeal with kidney problems but bore it all so patiently. Good that Alice Rogers could join you for the mini-retreat. Thanks for her letter enclosed with yours. I will drop her a note.

Today is the feast day for St. Joseph the Worker. It is good to take time out from all the work. My workers are putting the wood paneling on the upper inside walls of the cathedral. It is going much faster than the aluminum siding on the outside. The two carpenters I have doing the finishing work have been with me for a long time and are much faster than the two guys who did the aluminum.

The picture below was taken just a week and a half ago. It was graduation day for our 10th sewing course. The girls are showing me their table display of some of their works. These are some knitted items as you may notice. Since I have the knitting needles and yarn, knitting has become part of the course. The picture was taken by a local lad who has set up a business for himself. He takes pictures, goes to Mwanza by bus each week (100 miles away) , gets the film developed where they have 2 hours service and comes back the next day by bus. On May 3, the 11th sewing course will begin. The sewing classes have been very successful.

The rains stopped abruptly at the end of March. There was only a little over an inch in all of April which is very unusual because April is usually a very good month for rain. Fortunately many people have gotten good harvests anyway, especially those who planted early.

I hope that Fr.Duffy's skin cancer is under control. I haven't had any problems since I had the sore burned off behind my ear. I wear a hat with a brim now instead of the cap which leaves too much of the head exposed. I was happy to hear that you got 29 birthday good wishes. Even though this is very late, maybe you could consider this number 30. You have lots of friends who remember you which says something of your own interest in them...

Love and prayers,
Fr. Marvin

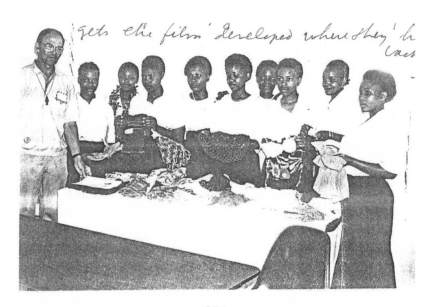

Queen of Peace Youth Center

Sunday, May 16, 1993

Dear Dorothy,

The youth center continues to be a busy place, attracting young and old alike. The new sewing course has 13 girls and is already beginning its 3rd week. At this very moment the Red Cross is holding a meeting in our auditorium. For outside groups like this we charge a small amount per day. They like to come here because of the park-like atmosphere which has become very attractive as the trees and shrubs have grown to maturity. There is nothing like it in Shinyanga. We now have put in outdoor seats made of stone and concrete - 3 different shapes for variety. The round one below was just finished about 10 days ago. There are lots of stones in this area which can be purchased cheaply and cement is readily available. Note the statue of St. Francis in the picture.

Last Sunday I had a vocation day for Buhangija School for both boys and girls. About 30 showed up. An African sister, Sr. Susanna helped me with one of the talks. She was just a little girl when I came to Tanzania in 1957. In fact, her father, Natalis Ndaki, was the catechist at Gula where I was first assigned to learn the Kisukuma language. He was my first teacher.

The outside of the cathedral is now complete. Everybody likes the color combination. The aluminum siding on the upper walls blends in nicely with the lower walls which are cement and plaster. The bell tower cross which is made of beams is now painted silver so that it shines in the sunlight. I hired a guy who is not afraid of heights to do the job. He is the same fellow who helped with the original construction. Eventually there will be 3 bells at the top of the tower which are supposed to come from the Bishop's friends in Germany.

On Sunday afternoon from 5 to 6:45 PM we usually have tennis for special guests. Some of the participants are Matthias Braun (a German working in Agriculture), Joseph (an African who works with Matthias), Miyuki (a young Japanese woman volunteer who teaches math at one of the high schools), Nick Ford (Peace Corp volunteer from Ohio who teaches at another school), Brother Cyril (Maryknoll), and of course, myself. Miyuki plays well and can keep up with the men. So we have kind of a United Nations here. Tennis continues to be very popular for the African youth who use the court from Monday to Friday.

Hi to Deb and all, with Love and prayers,
Fr. Marvin

We built these stone and cement seats outside the auditorium in the shade.

Students who came for a YCS (Young Christian Students) meeting.

(Bishop Sekwa's Brain Tumor Returns)

Dar es Salaam

July 1, 1993

Dear Dorothy,

Today is already the first day of July and a good time to write to you. Thanks much for your birthday letter of June 2 which arrived just before my birthday. We had a small party for my birthday - just Brother Kevin, Bishop Castor Sekwa and myself for an evening meal. Bishop Castor has not been well and so we wanted to make it relaxing for him. He walked over from his house about a block away, but barely made it. We had to help him in and out of the chair. His left side is becoming paralyzed again almost like it was before he had brain surgery several years ago. I was shocked to see how he had gone downhill since I had seen him about a week and a half before. Anyhow, he wanted to come for my birthday and made a great effort. I took him home in my pickup. Kevin and I helped him in and out of the car.

I left for Dar on Monday, June 28th. One of my good and faithful workers, Johnny Mwandu, traveled with me. We made the 600 mile trip in 2 days, staying overnight at the Catholic Church Social Center in the town of Sengida which is about half way. The road is very rough the first 300 miles, but my pickup continues to function well. We had no trouble except a cut tire from a rock which didn't go all the way through, so I didn't have to change it.

When I got to the Maryknoll house in Dar, Fr. Howie O'Brien had already received the message via radio call that bishop Castor had been flown by the flying doctor plane to Nairobi where he will undergo a cat-scan to see if the tumor is growing again in the brain. It doesn't look good for him at all and it seems to me that even if he lives for some time, he will be confined to a wheelchair. It seems sad - just as the conference center and cathedral are being completed. I am enclosing some pictures of the Cathedral. As you can see, most of the work is done now. Even all the pews are in.

Love and prayers,
Fr. Marvin

Working on the design behind the altar

I think it is good here to explain the great number of people who were involved in the building of the cathedral. First of all - there was the original architect whom I never met. Then there was the architect in Minneapolis, Jerry Rauenhorst, who modified the sanctuary. Then there was the Singh in Nairobi who was contracted to put up the beams. Actually he did not do the work. He subcontracted the work to a group of Africans who did the work. The leader of these men told me that the Singh never fully paid them. Maryknoll Brother, John Wohead, with his transit, helped lay out the location of the footings for the vertical beams so they would be in exactly the right position and correct level. There was another African contractor who put up the walls, put on the roof, poured the rough concrete etc. And lastly I came on the scene to supervise the finishing work. Because I did this, I saved the Bishop perhaps a couple hundred thousand dollars. We built the altar, for example, for a song. I supervised all the painting, most of the terrazzo floor, the parking lot, etc. I hired Joseph Ibrech to build the pews. He charged a bare minimum for his work.

Honestly, when I look back on what I had to do, I am truly amazed that I had the strength and the know-how to accomplish this task. My health was breaking down as the pages ahead will explain. My body and my mind were wearing out with all the stress and double duty which I was attempting to do together with my youth work. But somehow, I held out. The Cathedral was blessed on May 18, 1994. The following month I would be 66 years old. In May of 1994 I went to the U.S. on Sabbatical to get a rest and to regain my strength. I was to leave Africa for good just before my 69th birthday.

These above pictures were taken in May 1993. In the upper picture the terrazzo floor is quite clear. We used two different colors of pebbles. The reddish color was used to form a cross upon which the altar rests. We also used two different colors in the main body of the church so the aisle would be distinct. The main altar, the Blessed Sacrament altar, the podium, were all built in my little workshop at the Youth Center. The wood paneling which I sent over in the container, made these jobs relatively easy. Also notice the upper walls to the left and to the right. These also were covered with paneling. The crucifix was a gift from Maryknoll, taken from our novitiate in Hingham, Mass., which was sold.

Dar es Salaam

July 7, 1993, 8:45 PM

Dear Dorothy,

I want to send you a short note before I leave Dar for Shinyanga. I plan to leave early tomorrow morning with Johnny Mwandu, my worker who drove up with me.

Our Bishop, Castor Sekwa, was operated on today in Nairobi hospital. He was flown there a few days ago by the flying doctor. The brain tumor has grown again. Fr. Dick Hochwalt called earlier this evening from Shinyanga and said that he received a call from Nairobi that the operation was still going on after 6 hours. So it must be very difficult and very complicated.

I have had a nice time here in Dar. Sr. Ursula returned from Germany and I had a chance to visit their convent several times. This afternoon I had a mass for their community - 3 African sisters, Sr. Ursula and Sr. Margarita, a German sister who is 71 years young and still going strong out here.

I hope all goes well. I see on the news (we have satellite T.V.) that the Mississippi is still rising and the flooding is getting worse.

Greetings to all, love and prayers,
Fr. Marvin

Something Crazy Happens

On our trip from Dar to Shinyanga, on day one, Johnny Mwandu and I got as far as Sengida which was about 350 miles. I found a hotel which was a little on the seedy side. I thought it best if we were together and not in separate hotels. Looking back on what happened, I should have put him up in a good hotel with me instead of trying to save money. We found something to eat which was not all that great and turned in for the night. At 5 AM in the morning there was a loud knocking at my door. The voice on the other side said, "This is the police...Open up". When I opened the door a police man in a long raincoat came barging in. He looked around and abruptly left. I couldn't figure out what he wanted. There were three or four other policemen with him, one being a woman. In a few minutes it all became clear to me. He was after the foreigner who was with an African girl prostitute. The guy was in the room next to me. They barged in there too and accused the guy of corrupting their African girls. I am sure they got the bribe they were looking for and then left the guy and the girl in peace. Johnny Mwandu woke up too. I said to Johnny that we may as well get going on our safari because I could never get back to sleep again after all that commotion. I was exhausted even before we started and was totally wiped out when we reached Shinyanga 12 hours later. Johnny was not a driver. See next letter....

Nairobi

July 25, 1993

Dear Dorothy,

You are probably surprised to hear from me from Nairobi. Actually I didn't expect to come here, but about a week ago I experienced chest pains and shortness of breath and so I decided I had better get this checked out, especially considering all the heart problems in our family.

On Tuesday, July 20th, I drove to Mwanza (100 miles from Shinyanga) taking with me one of my workers, Johnny Mwandu - just in case I had a flat tire and needed help changing it. Arrangements had already been made to get the plane from Mwanza to Nairobi. The Protestants (African Inland Church) have a couple of small planes that fly regularly between Mwanza and Nairobi and they let us go with them for $120 one way which is very cheap. I arrived in Mwanza at

10:15 A.M. and got the plane at 12:30. I left my pickup with Fr. John Eyble, a Maryknoll priest who works at Bugando hospital in Mwanza and gave Johnny Mwandu money to return to Shinyanga by bus. The flight to Nairobi is only 2 hours. We flew in a twin engine Cessna which had about 8 passengers.

I took a cab from the airport to the Maryknoll house. The next morning I went to see Dr. Silverstein, an American heart specialist at Nairobi hospital. I had seen him before in 1988. He remembered me. I was checked out quite thoroughly - blood pressure, cardiogram and stress test. I ran on the treadmill all hooked up to the cardiogram and blood pressure instruments and did very well. I ran for about 10 minutes and everything checked out as normal. I was diagnosed with hyperventilation, which mimics a heart problem. It is caused by too much stress and not enough rest. An Indian doctor who is assistant to Dr. Silverstein asked me what I do. When I explained to him my many involvements, he said, "I have a brother just like you. He thinks he can solve all the problems in the world." He suggested that I cut my schedule in half and I will be all right.

I think the Lord wants me up here anyways. Right after my tests I went to another part of the hospital to see our Bishop who had brain surgery on July 7 and had not been doing too well. He had lapsed into a coma about 2 days after the operation. When I saw him, there had been no change. This was July 21. The coma was caused by swelling of the brain which often follows these operations. At this point it did not seem that he would survive.

For several days I did very little except rest and take it easy and just like the doctor anticipated, the shortness of breath and uneasiness in the chest began to disappear.

On July 24, I went back to Nairobi hospital to check on the Bishop. By good luck I ran into Dr. Risso just as he was coming out of the Bishop's ward. He knows me from the last operation that the Bishop had three and a half years ago. Dr. Risso spent about a half hour with me explaining the whole situation. He said when he removed the first rumor three and a half years ago, he found it benign and did not expect it to grow back again for at least 10 years. To make a long story short, he said that if the brain swelling goes down there is a chance that the Bishop could recover although he could be partially paralyzed on the left side.

We then went over to see the Bishop. I was surprised to see that he had improved. He was awake although showed no sign of recognizing me. But he was able to respond to some simple commands of the doctor, like moving his fingers which was a hopeful sign. For days there had been no communication whatsoever.

I will stop in to see the Bishop again in a couple of days and will let you know in my next letter if there is any improvement. I expect to be here for one more week to make sure everything is all right with my health. I hope that all goes well and that it has finally stopped raining.

Love and prayers,

Fr. Marvin

Nairobi

July 29, 1993

Dear Dorothy,

This afternoon I am going out to Mwangaza which is the Jesuit retreat house on the edge of the city of Nairobi. I want to spend a few days in silence and prayer before going back to Tanzania. I will be there until Monday morning, Aug. 2. The small plane which flies to Mwanza, the southern port of lake Victoria where I left my pickup, leaves at 8:00 A.M. Wilson Airport which handles all these small planes, is only about a 10 minute drive from the retreat house. A Maryknoll priest, Fr. Richard Smith, who works with the Jesuits at the retreat house, said he would drive me to the airport.

Fr. Ernie Brunelle, who just got back from leave in the U.S. will be with me. Ernie has really had a lot of heart problems - 2 bye passes. He is on all kinds of medications - blood thinners, artery dilators, cholesterol diminishers, etc. It doesn't seem to phase him. Ernie has helped me with the youth work this past year, especially teaching religion in the secondary schools, which is not an easy job.

Fr. Ernie was in to see the Bishop at Nairobi hospital yesterday. There was some improvement. The Bishop could move his fingers and Ernie thinks the Bishop recognized him. We will stop in again today on the way to the retreat house.

I am feeling good again. As far as the doctors can tell, I have no health problems, which is a blessing for a person my age. I want to send you this note from Nairobi since it is much easier to write when I have the leisure. Hope the rains have finally slowed down in the Midwest.

Love and prayers,
Fr. Marvin.

Footnote:

A book I had with me during retreat was a big help. The title was "The Memory Palaces of Matteo Ricci" It was about the fascinating life of Fr. Matteo Ricci, an Italian Jesuit who worked in China in the early 1700 C. He was extremely talented and very much in demand as a speaker because he knew the Chinese language so well. He had a severe headache after one of his talks and when a fellow priest said that with a little rest it would go away, Matteo said - "No it won't. The problem I have is that I have too much to do." He died shortly afterwards, most likely from an aneurism. I took this message to heart and resolved to slow down.

Queen of Peace Youth Center

Monday, August 9, 1993

Dear Dorothy,

Many thanks for your letters of July 7 and 28th. That was a good thing you did to visit Margaret's relatives, especially that she may feel your support in seeking out those lost relationships which are very important to her.

I arrived back from Nairobi a week ago today. Fr. Ernie and I had a nice flight on the "Maf" plane (protestant organization) from Nairobi to Mwanza. Ordinarily it is a two hour flight, but they had a 12 seater turbo-prop which made the flight in 1 hour and 20 minutes. Fr. Peter La Jacq's driver met us at the airport with my pickup which I had left at his place. Fr. Ernie and I drove the 100 miles from Mwanza to Shinyanga and we were back in time for supper, Monday evening, August 2.

I really enjoyed my 3 1/2 day stay at the "Mwangaza" Jesuit retreat house. They have magnificent grounds with a beautiful view of the Ngong hills. Even though it is a busy place (There were 30 making retreats when I arrived) it is still very peaceful and restful mainly because strict silence is observed at all times, which was just what I was looking for.

On Sunday Fr. Dick Smith, who works at the retreat house, drove me to Nairobi hospital. I interrupted my retreat for an hour and a half to see the Bishop. He was able to recognize me, but that was about all. He could not speak and his left side is paralyzed, but at least he had made some progress. It will be a long road to recovery.

Brother Kevin had everything under control here at the Youth Center. The building work is winding down now. I am going to take it much easier which is important if I want to stay in good health.

Good to hear the rains are finally slowing down....Greetings to all....

Love and prayers,
Fr. Marvin

Footnote:

Margaret was Dorothy's adopted daughter. She had discovered some of her relatives from her birth mother and needed Dorothy's encouragement to pursue these relationships.

Queen of Peace Youth Center

Tues. August 31, 1993

Dear Dorothy,

Today, the last day of August, is a Muslim holiday, the birthday of Muhammad. It is something akin to our Christmas,-no work and no school today. I spent the morning working on my Toyota pickup. The muffler finally gave out and fell off. As the noise was increasing the past few weeks, I knew it was a matter of time before it was finished completely. You can't buy a complete ready-made muffler here in Shinyanga and so you use various parts and make up a new one. There are a lot of places that weld the pieces together for you. I had a couple of my workers help me. They are young and agile and can crawl under the car better than I can. My Toyota is a little over 6 years old now, but still in very good condition. When it is washed, it still looks like new - no rust or body damage.

We have some good news on our Bishop Castor Sekwa. Fr. Dick Hochwalt went to Nairobi to see him. Dick called here the other night and said the Bishop is doing well. Dr. Risso, who did the surgery, can't understand how the Bishop could improve so rapidly. He is gaining some use of his left side which was not expected. He is actually walking with the aid of a walker. His speech has returned to normal. In fact, the doctor thinks the Bishop could return to Shinyanga by the end of September if he should so wish.

The finish work in the cathedral is going well. We are varnishing the sedila (presiding priest's chair), have assembled the baptismal font (made of wood mahogany) and are building the frames for the Stations of the Cross. Joseph Ibrecht, who has the biggest workshop in town, has the confessionals assembled. (Joseph made all the pews in his workshop) In a week's time all these things should be in the cathedral. I have workers putting in the sidewalk which will lead from the sacristy door to the front steps - which will be very important for processions on the big days when the Bishop and priests vest in the sacristy and process along the side of the church in order to enter by the front door.

My health has been O.K. The big thing is to take it easy. I try to take at least a half hour nap after lunch and also a short nap before supper. It has helped my overall condition a lot.

Love and Greetings to all,
Fr. Marvin

My two carpenters who worked for me for several years.

Above top picture: Fastening the confessional in plae
Lower picture: working on the priest's chair called the sedila

Showing the new baptismal fount to my good friend Joseph Ibrecht who was such a big help to me. (taken Sept. 1993)

Johnny Mwandu - worked for me for many years taking care of the grounds. He cut the grass with our imported lawn mower and also learned how to prune trees.

We built a high scaffolding to reach the upper branches. If you look closely, you will see me on the picture running.

On the right - Edward, the watchman of the Bishop's compound - a very fine man. I am sorry I don't have a frontal picture of him.

Queen of Peace Youth Center

Sunday, Oct. 3, 1993

Dear Dorothy,

Thanks for your letter of Sept. 13 which arrived on Sept. 28, taking about 2 weeks which is faster than usual. I am happy to hear that you could get together with Fr. John Lange, Alice Rogers, and friends. John is special and has a great way with people. He even took time out to see Marlys and Floyd which says something. John is back in Nairobi now.

I wrote a check for $3000 from my account at Norwest and deposited it in the Cathedral account here. I want to use the money which has come in this past year for the work here. Right now I am the only one signing the checks on the Cathedral account since I am in charge of finishing the building. Eventually I will turn this account over to the new pastor who has not yet been named. Perhaps the bishop will wait until he returns before he appoints someone there. The check will take 3 weeks to clear. Nothing happens fast here. Even to cash a check at the local bank takes at least a half hour. The checks I deposit in my youth center account coming from Musoma, our regional headquarters, cannot be drawn upon for one month since it takes that long for the checks to clear.

The work on the cathedral is moving steadily along. I am now concentrating on the parking lot. We are putting up an 18 inch wall to separate the parking lot from the church - just high enough so people can sit on it. I have also started the gates which will allow cars to come from the rear of the parking lot rather than having to come from the front of the church which is where the people walk. It is safer that way. There is quite a bit of work to do in the parking lot which will take at least a month. I am happy the inside work is done now.

I haven't heard much news on the bishop but will find out more when Fr. Hugh gets back. My health is O.K. I seem to tire quicker than what is normal for me and so I take one or two naps every day. I plan to take 2 weeks off in December.

Love and Greetings to All,

Fr. Marvin

One of the last things to be done at the cathedral was the parking lot. I put in a series of diamond squares so that cars would automatically have to park at an angle in an orderly way. We planted niem trees in each square so that there would be shade for the vehicles. The niem tree was special because it did not lose its leaves in the long dry season. Also they grew very quickly. The bottom picture was taken a few years after the cathedral was blessed

There is more to write about, but I think it best to summarize the events that followed.

The Cathedral was blessed on May 18, 1994. This was the 20th anniversary of Bishop Castor Sekwa's ordination to the Episcopacy. He had recovered sufficiently from his 2nd brain surgery so that he could return to the diocese. He was very handicapped, however. He could walk with difficulty and very slowly with a walker. Shortly after, I don't remember the exact date, Bishop Aloysius Balina was asked to be the administrator even though he had his hands full with his own diocese of Geita to the North of Shinyanga diocese. I had informed Bishop Castor that I would not be present for the blessing, and wanted to leave for the U.S. and home leave by mid-May., It was better that way. The one who should receive credit for all that had been done was the Bishop himself. Also there were many others who had participated in the building of the Cathedral. My very good friend, Fr. Richard Hochwalt, who was the Bishop's Vicar General, asked the Bishop to write a letter to me in appreciation for what I had done. I am sure that Fr. Hochwalt did most of the composing although the Bishop meant every word of the letter. The Bishop had asked me to have a card printed with the picture of Cathedral which he could put into the invitation for the blessing. I had one prepared in Nairobi. The official title of the Cathedral was "Mama Mwenye Huruma" (Mother of Mercy).

SHINYANGA CATHEDRAL
MAMA MWENYE HURMA
The Flamboyant trees were in full bloom when I took this picture.

N 3651/94/211-vol XII

DIOCESE OF SHINYANGA
P.O. Box 47 — Phone 2068
SHINYANGA, TANZANIA

6 May 1994

Reverend Marvin F. Deutsch, M.M.
Youth Centre

Dear Father Marvin,

My greetings and best wishes for the Home-leave safari you are soon to begin.

You have done so much to develop the Diocese, you have worked and given of yourself and your material means also without stint, you took up the planning and construction of the complex that Ngokolo now is - the Hostel, the Offices and Conference Room, and over all the Cathedral.

With quiet efficiency, in good humour always, you carried out the construction, and I must not forget, of the Youth Centre itself, and the facilities there, of the Hostel and Offices, and always of the Cathedral. I want to thank you. I need to express my admiration and gratitude for this work. Ngokolo now stands as it is because you entered in the work and carried it through to completion. I owe this gratitude and this admiration, and the entire Diocese owes it you.
Now you are to begin a well deserved Home-leave. Your work has at times brought you to exhaustion, yet you continued on without complaint, always looking to the goal, always ready to assist and to do. Thank you!

This work is so close to my heart, especially the Cathedral. I am glad to see it ready now for its dedication, and I regret that you will not be with us on that day when I shall surely make public acknowledgment of the essential role you played. I had hoped that you would be there but accept that you wish to begin at once your Leave. Go then with my blessing, with my gratitude, with my trust that you will return to Shinyanga once more ready to continue your beloved apostolate to the christian education of youth, for in all the work of construction and the like you never forgot nor left aside this essential apostolate.

We are proud of what is at Ngokolo now, and you must also be very proud and recognize the magnificent work you have accomplished. All this is because you were ready to take on the task of completion and making ready all that is there, and again especially the Cathedral.

Speak to your family, to your friends in America, and tell them of what you have completed and accomplished and tell them of our gratitude and appreciation of you! Let them know for sure that there is a great role here for Missionaries, that we need and want and love them for their vocation and their zeal and dedication, of whom you are such a fine example.

With my Blessing and prayers and wishing you a happy Home-Leave,
I am,

Sincerely yours in Christ,

Castor Sekwa, D.D.
Bishop of Shinyanga

(I am making a second copy of this letter which will follow
because the original is quite light to read)

N 3651/94/211-vol XII

DIOCESE OF SHINYANGA
P.O. Box 47 – Phone 2068
SHINYANGA, TANZANIA

6 May 1994

Reverend Marvin F. Deutsch, M.M. Youth Centre
Dear Father Marvin,

My greetings and best wishes for the Home-leave
safari you are soon to begin.

You have done so much to develop the Diocese, you
have worked and given of yourself and your material
means also without stint, you took up the planning
and construction of the complex that Ngokolo now is
the Hostel, the Offices and Conference Room, and over
all the Cathedral.

With quiet efficiency, in good humour always, you carried out the construction, and I must not forget, of the Youth Centre itself, and the facilities there, of the Hostel and Offices, and always of the Cathedral. I want to thank you. I need to express my admiration and gratitude for this work. Ngokolo now stands as it is because you entered into the work and carried it through to completion. I owe this gratitude and this admiration, and the entire Diocese owes it (to) you.

Now you are to begin a well deserved Home-leave. Your work has at times brought you to exhaustion, yet you continued on without complaint, always looking to the goal, always ready to assist and to do. Thank you!

This work is so close to my heart, especially the Cathedral. I am glad to see it ready now for its dedication, and I regret that you will not be with us on that day when I shall surely make public acknowledgment of the essential role you played. I had hoped that you would be there but accept that you wish to begin at once your Leave. Go then with my blessing, with my gratitude, with my trust that you will return to Shinyanga once more ready to continue your beloved apostolate to the christian education of youth, for in all the work of construction and the like you never forgot nor left aside this essential apostolate.

We are proud of what is at Ngokolo now, and you must also be very proud and recognize the magnificent work you have accomplished. All this is because you were ready to take on the task of completion and making ready all that is there, and again especially the Cathedral.

Speak to your family, to your friends in America, and tell them of what you have completed and accomplished and tell them of our gratitude and appreciation of you! Let them know for sure that there is a great role here for Missionaries, that we need and want and love them for their vocation and their zeal and dedication, of whom you are such a fine example.

With my Blessing and prayers and wishing you a happy Home-Leave, I am,
                    Sincerely yours in Christ,
                    Castor Sekwa, D.D.
                    Bishop of Shinyanga

In the spring of 1994, Brother Kevin and I carried on with our youth work. I was happy to have the construction work behind me. In April we had over 100 students for the Holy Week retreat. On Holy Saturday night Brother Kevin and I were eating our evening meal about an hour before we would begin the Easter vigil service. There was a call from our gate. I went out to see who it was. It was a Belgian family coming from Rwanda. They said they were on vacation and on their way to the Serengeti Plains to see the animals. They wanted to park their vehicle in our compound for security reasons. We told them that they were very welcome and could even use one of our guest houses for the night. Since they were Catholics they asked if they could attend the Easter Vigil Service with the students, which they did. On Easter Sunday morning they left. We got a nice picture before they left (below). It was just a couple of days later, April 6th, that all hell broke loose in Rwanda. The genocide had begun. The Belgian family were very fortunate to have left before this terrible event. I heard from them several weeks later. They sent me a postcard from Belgium stating how fortunate they were to get out of Rwanda before the massacre began.

Brother Kevin and I with the Belgian family - April 3, 1994, Easter Sunday morning.

The following picture has two men not in the bottom picture: front row - far left - Fr. Leo Kennedy and in the middle - Fr. Mike Snyder. It was taken at the Youth Center, 1994.

The above picture - **Back row**: Fr. Paul Fagan, Fr. Don Sybertz, Brother Kevin Dargan Fr. Dave Smith, Fr. Lou Quinn, Fr. Richard Hochwalt, Fr.Lou Bayless,

Front row: Brother John Wohead, Fr. Dan Ohmann, Brother Cyril Vellicig, Fr. John, Fr. Marv Deutsch, Fr. Herb Gappa, Fr. Ernie Brunelle

In 1996 Fr. Philemon Machagija was assigned to assist me at Queen of Peace Youth Center. He is pictured with me above. Brother Kevin had been assigned to Musoma. My letter to Dorothy explains:

Queen of Peace Youth Center

Easter, Thursday, 1996

Dear Dorothy,

The time is going by quickly. Easter is over already. The Holy Week retreat was a great success. 109 students representing 13 schools attended.

Fr. Philemon Machagija is the priest assigned here to run the center. The Bishop asked me to come back in December and continue on here. Fr. Philemon will be administrator while I am gone. I would prefer to hand everything over but they want the transition to go slowly. So I just hope that I stay in good health to continue on here for part of next year, something like this year.

Thanks for the info on the $1000 gift from the Kleves. I am writing to them today. They are very generous.

We have had some good rains - about 7 inches this month which is not yet half over. The crops thus will be fair which is encouraging. At first it looked like famine..

Happy Springtime....
> *Love and prayers,*
> *Fr. Marvin*

Fr. Machagija was a very fine African priest. He was a big help to me especially because he liked to teach religion in the Secondary schools. It was always hard to get people to teach. I went home to the States again in late May. My health was poor. I just didn't have energy. Before I left in May, 1996, I went to say goodbye to my good friend, Bishop Castor Sekwa. He had been inactive for some time. When I saw him, he was very weak and could only talk with a whisper. We had worked together for a long time and were good friends. I was happy I could do so much for him. It was amazing that he had so much confidence in me. Within 2 weeks of my departure, Bishop Castor died - June 4, 1996. His body rests beneath the floor in a corner of the sanctuary in the cathedral which was his pride and joy. In a way our careers coincided. I was ordained two years before him. His picture taken for his 25th anniversary to the priesthood is below.

YUBILEE

ASKOFU C. SEKWA
JIMBO LA SHINYANGA

Date of birth	March 28, 1927
Ordained	August 15, 1959
Became Bishop	May 18, 1975
Died	June 4, 1996

I returned to Tanzania in December of 1996. I had been living and working for several months at a retreat house near Waconia, Minnesota. My sister, Dorothy, died on July 29, 1996. It was an untimely death. She and I had gone to visit our elderly aunt, Sr. Leonarda, at Yankton, South Dakota in late June. While there, Dorothy fell and broke her hip. She was operated on there at Sacred Heart hospital. After about 2 weeks, her insurance became invalid because she was out of state. I went to pick her up and brought her back to her home in Minneapolis where her insurance would be good. She fell again which required another operation. She did not survive the operation.

When I returned to Tanzania in December, I no longer had a pen pal to exchange letters with. And so I have no written record of my activities from December 1996 to May of 1997 when I left Africa for good.

Chapter VI

My Last Job: Spiritual Director for Young African Seminarians

When I returned to the youth center, I found that Fr..Machagija was doing a very fine job teaching in the schools and running the center. Another job opened up for me. For several years the dioceses in Tanzania had a special year called a spiritual formation year which had been added on to the seminary training period. Pope John Paul II had requested this of the African Bishops primarily because of the failures of some of the priests regarding celibacy. This special year was not carried out in the seminary but locally in the diocese. In our diocese there were 7 young seminarians who had finished two years of college who were in the program. Fr. Amadeus who was the chaplain of Shinyanga Secondary school (My old stamping grounds from 1982-1988) was in charge of the program. He did not like the job and did not feel qualified. I was asked by Bishop Balina to take it over. I readily agreed. There was a very small guest house there which had been built by Fr. Dan Cashman a few years earlier. I moved into it and immediately began to teach and work with the young men.

Because my studies in Rome in 1981-82 centered on spirituality, I had no problem in fulfilling this assignment. I enjoyed it very much. I taught several classes every day, prayed and worked with the seminarians. We had manual labor almost every day. One of our jobs was to repair the road coming to the school which was in pretty bad shape. I also had supper every day with the seminarians and Fr. Amadeus who took care of the administration. The meals were very African. One evening we had rice and beans. The next evening we had ugali and beans. (Ugali is cooked corn flour). The next night we had rice and beans. It was the same thing over and over again. It was quite monotonous, but I didn't mind because I used to go to the market by bicycle and get fruit. to supplement this diet.

My central theme was helping the seminarians develop a personal relationship and friendship with Jesus Christ. Learning theology in the seminary was a training of the mind. I saw the spiritual formation year as a training of the heart. One who loves Christ doesn't want to do anything which would jeopardize that relationship. And of course, this is what sin does. Prayer, self denial and visits to the Blessed Sacrament are essential.

My last days in Africa were spent with these young men helping them in their spiritual formation year. I enjoyed it very much. It was a good note to leave on.

About the Author

Fr. Marvin Deutsch grew up in South Minneapolis. He is from a large family of 8 children. He attended two years of College at St. Thomas College in St. Paul, Minnesota before entering Maryknoll. He was ordained in 1957 and assigned to Tanganyika (today called Tanzania) where he worked as a missionary for over 30 years. For the first 6 years he worked in a remote area of Shinyanga diocese doing primary evangelization, that is, introducing Christianity where it did not exist before. For about 25 years he worked with youth, first in the capital city of Dar es Salaam, and later in the diocese of Shinyanga where he first started out. He set up youth centers in both places.

On his 25th anniversary as a priest he took a sabbatical, studying at the universities of the Angelicum and Gregorian in Rome. It was the intellectual highlight of his life. He took courses in spiritual direction, retreat methods, the problem of the 7 capital sins, the epistles of St. Paul and the greatest subject of all, the Vatican Council's teaching on Divine Revelation.   When Fr. Deutsch retired from missionary work in 1997, he began giving retreats and doing spiritual direction in the Archdiocese of St. Paul and Minneapolis.

In 2004 he moved to the Maryknoll retirement home in Los Altos, California where he began writing his books: "Strangers and Sojourners No longer", Essays and Homilies for our Times", and "Letters from Africa". The latter, (composed of 3 books), was made possible because of over 1000 letters written to his mother which she saved.   Four of his books have been published in paperback by Amazon: "To Find Jesus is to Find the Meaning of Life", "The Marvel of God's Life Within Us", "The Role of Mary in the Modern World for Our Salvation" and this book, "The Adventures of a Maryknoll Priest bringing the Good News of Christ to African Youth."

Fr. Marvin Deutsch's Books on Amazon

- **The Marvel of God's Life Within Us**
  - Available:
    - Paperback book (2019)
    - Kindle ebook (2018)

- ## A Missionary's letters from Africa: Part 1, 1956 - 1963
  - Available:
    - Kindle ebook (2018)

- ## A Missionary's letters from Africa: Part 2, 1981 - 1997
  - Available:
    - Kindle ebook (2018)

- ## Role of Mary in the Modern World for our Salvation
  - Available:
    - Kindle ebook (2018)
    - Paperback book (2020)

- ## Essays and Homilies, Witnessing to the Truth
  - Available:
    - Kindle ebook (2018)

- **To Find Jesus is to find the Meaning of Life**
  - Available:
    - Paperback book (2019)
    - Kindle ebook (2019)